USA TODAY'S DEBATE: VOICES AND PERSPECTIVES

GREEN ENERGY

Crucial Gains or Economic Strains?

Matt Doeden

Twenty-First Century Books · Minneapolis

Twenty-First Century Books
A division of Lerner Publishing Group, Inc.
241 First Avenue North
Minneapolis, MN 55401 U.S.A.

Website address: www.lernerbooks.com

The publisher wishes to thank Ben Nussbaum and Phil Pruitt of USA TODAY for their help in preparing this book.

Library of Congress Cataloging-in-Publication Data

Doeden, Matt.
    Green energy : crucial gains or economic strains? / by Matt Doeden.
       p.   cm. — (USA TODAY's debate: voices and perspectives)
    Includes bibliographical references and index.
    ISBN 978–0–7613–5112–2 (lib. bdg. : alk. paper)
    1. Power resources—United States. 2. Power resources—Moral and ethical aspects—United States. 3. Energy policy—Moral and ethical aspects—United States. 4. Renewable energy sources—United States. I. Title.
    TJ163.25.U6D64 2010
    333.79'4—dc22   2009026121

Manufactured in the United States of America
1 – DP – 12/15/09

CONTENTS

Regular
Gasoline

4 8 8 $\frac{9}{10}$

Plus
Gasoline

4 9 9 $\frac{9}{10}$

V-Power®
Gasoline

5 0 9 $\frac{9}{10}$

Diesel #2

5 3 9 $\frac{9}{10}$

TOYO

scion

INTRODUCTION

The Search for Renewable Energy

IN THE SUMMER OF 2008, THE PRICE OF GASOLINE seemed to be on everyone's mind. People were used to paying $2 per gallon ($.53 per liter) or even a bit more. But in 2008, gas prices climbed to $3 and then $4 per gallon ($.79 and $1.05 per liter) and higher.

That year oil prices surged higher than $140 per barrel—more than double the average 2007 price and triple the average 2004 price. Gasoline is made from oil. So the price of gas surged alongside the price of oil.

High gasoline prices had far-reaching consequences. Food and other goods shipped by truck got more expensive. Fuel prices for jet airplanes went up, so airlines had to charge more for tickets. Many people struggled with the cost of filling their gas tanks. Some folks sold their jewelry and other valuables just so they could get to work. The already struggling U.S. economy could ill afford the extra strain.

Left: Gas prices reached their highest in summer 2008 in states such as California, where prices neared $5 per gallon ($1.32 per liter).

Many people complained and worried about gasoline prices. Some pressed for more U.S. oil drilling.

But others took a different viewpoint. They said that the shocking gasoline prices were a badly needed wake-up call. Americans were addicted to oil. Gasoline-burning vehicles released pollution that was wreaking havoc in the environment. Furthermore, U.S. dependence on oil imported from foreign countries threatened national security. The nation's economy relied heavily on a resource it did not control. It was time to develop energy alternatives seriously. A new "green" energy economy would lead to a cleaner, safer future.

Green energy is energy that creates little or no pollution and comes from renewable resources. Renewable resources are ones that nature can replace. Green energy includes a wide range of technologies. Solar and wind power are the best known. But other technologies—such as those that harness the energy in plant matter, moving water,

Above: This oil refinery is in Kirkuk, Iraq. Many people are concerned about the international entanglements that accompany U.S. oil dependence.

and Earth itself—are also important. Even nuclear power, once considered an enemy of the environment, is gaining acceptance as a cleaner alternative to fossil fuels (coal, oil, and natural gas).

THE DEBATE

The debate over the future of energy in the United States is complicated. Must Americans find new ways to power their cars, heat their homes, and generate their electricity? If so, what might those alternatives be? Can renewable resources produce enough power to supply the world? Is nuclear power the future?

Developing new technology is expensive. Can the United States—and the world—afford to make the transition from fossil fuels to green energy? Will this transition drain the economy or boost it? How soon can a transition occur?

Most people agree that the current U.S. energy system will not work for the long term. But even though people agree on the need for change, they don't agree on how and when that change should happen.

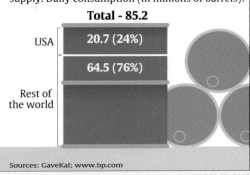

USA TODAY Snapshots®

Oil: USA's lifeblood

The U.S. has fewer than 5% of the world's 6.7 billion people but uses nearly 25% of the daily oil supply. Daily consumption (in millions of barrels):

Total - 85.2

USA   20.7 (24%)

64.5 (76%)

Rest of the world

Sources: GaveKal; www.bp.com

By Anne R. Carey and Adrienne Lewis, USA TODAY, 2008

CHAPTER ONE

A Crude History of Energy

ENERGY TECHNOLOGIES AND CIVILIZATION HAVE developed side by side. About eight hundred thousand years ago, humans figured out how to control and use fire. For millennia after that, people burned wood, dung, animal fat, and other fuels for warmth, light, and cooking. As early as five thousand years ago, the residents of Mesopotamia (modern Iraq) were burning crude oil (unrefined or unprocessed oil).

People eventually discovered that different sorts of energy exist. All forms of energy fall into two main categories: kinetic (motion) energy and potential (stored) energy. The movement of water and wind are two examples of kinetic energy. People learned to harness this energy through devices such as waterwheels and windmills. These devices transfer the kinetic energy of moving water or wind to machinery such as a grain

Left: Built in the fourteenth century, this *noria* (waterwheel) on the Orontes River in Syria supplied water to nearby farms and homes. The flowing river turned the noria. Meanwhile, containers on the noria's rim scooped up water and dumped it into the channel on top of the aqueduct (*far left*). Gravity then made the water in the aqueduct flow downhill through a network of channels to area residents.

mill. The energy stored within a material, such as wood or coal, is an example of potential energy. Burning such a material is one way to release the stored energy.

In the 600s B.C., the ancient Greeks found that an amber rod rubbed with a silk cloth attracted certain objects. They had discovered static electricity.

The term *electricity*, however, didn't exist until the A.D. 1600s. In 1600 English physician William Gibson used the Latin term *electricus*, which means "like amber," to compare the attractive powers of magnets and amber. In 1646 another English physician, Thomas Browne, coined the term *electricity*.

In 1752 American Benjamin Franklin tested his theory that lightning and electricity are the same thing. He tied a kite to one end of a long string and a metal key to the other end. Franklin then let the kite soar high in a stormy sky. In time,

Above: Amber is fossilized tree resin, or hardened sap from prehistoric trees. People often use amber to make jewelry.

Above: This nineteenth-century French engraving shows Alessandro Volta with his battery.

he noticed the fibers of the string standing on end. They were picking up an electrical charge from the storm clouds. Franklin touched his knuckle to the key. He saw a spark and felt a shock. This simple experiment proved that electricity, which was little understood at the time, was the force that drove lightning.

A decade later, Swedish physicist Johan Wilcke invented the first electric battery. Italian Alessandro Volta later improved the design and for this reason often gets credit for the invention. In the early 1800s, Great Britain's Humphry Davy invented the first effective electric lamp. Humankind's energy use would never be the same.

THE ENERGY REVOLUTION

Electricity wasn't the only form of energy people studied in the 1700s. Humans also developed the modern steam engine during that century. The technology took off in 1769 when James Watt built and patented his famous steam engine. This engine soon powered factories, mining and farm equipment, ships, trains, and other machines.

Coal furnaces powered the engines, creating huge plumes of sooty smoke. Coal was messy,

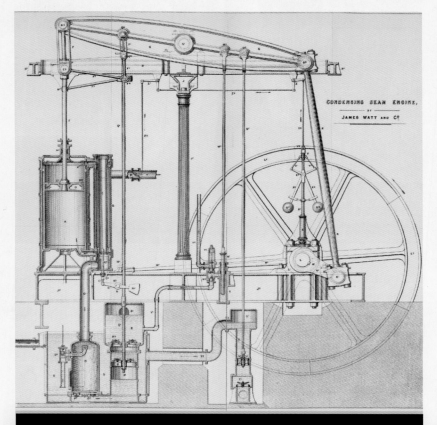

CONDENSING BEAM ENGINE,
BY
JAMES WATT AND CO

Above: This drawing from James Watt and Company shows the structure of his famous steam engine.

What's a Watt?

People measure the production and use of electricity in watts, a unit whose name honors inventor James Watt. A lightbulb needs about 40 watts. A car needs about 25,000 watts. A kilowatt is 1,000 watts. A megawatt is 1 million watts. A gigawatt is 1 billion watts.

Above: The watt is named after James Watt, in honor of his important eighteenth-century inventions.

but no other fuel widely available then packed quite the same energy punch. People began using coal for heating and to power the earliest electrical generators. A new age in energy began: the age of fossil fuels.

All three types of fossil fuels—coal, oil, and natural gas—had formed from organic material (plants and animals) over millions of years. The still-forming Earth had buried the organic material under rock, soil, and water. The material had decayed under extreme heat and pressure. This process had condensed the organic matter into substances crammed with stored chemical energy.

Fossil Fuels

For centuries, people have relied on fossil fuels—mainly coal and oil—to supply energy. Most fossil fuels began forming more than three hundred million years ago, during a time called the Carboniferous period.

Trees and many other kinds of plants flourished during this time. As they died, many sank to the bottoms of lakes and oceans. The dead plants formed a spongy substance called peat. Layer upon layer of rock eventually covered the peat, putting it under tremendous pressure. Over millions of years, this pressure changed the peat into coal. Oil and natural gas formed through a similar process. They formed from the remains of sea life—mainly single-celled creatures such as algae or zooplankton.

Above: Trains carry loads of coal through Nebraska.

Above: A derrick pumps oil from the ground beneath a Kansas wheat field. Oil and other fossil fuels usually lie far beneath Earth's surface.

Fossil fuels grew more and more important over time. They were plentiful and cheap. The abundance of cheap fuel—especially coal—spurred a huge expansion of industry in the late 1700s and early 1800s. The Industrial Revolution (a combination of major changes in agriculture, manufacturing, mining, and transportation) gave birth to the modern world economy.

HOOKED ON OIL

Coal reigned for about two centuries as the world's dominant fossil fuel. Oil, or petroleum, played only a small part in humankind's energy use—mainly in the form of kerosene heating oil. But change was under way.

Throughout the 1800s, European and U.S. inventors had been perfecting the internal combustion engine (ICE). These engines work by burning fuel inside the engine itself. Fuel burns inside small cylinders in the engine. The energy released by the burning fuel makes a piston move. That kinetic energy can then turn the wheels of a vehicle.

Inventors found that gasoline, a product refined from crude oil, was the perfect fuel for the ICE. In the late 1800s, European companies began making gasoline-powered automobiles. In the early 1900s, U.S. factories started making cars on assembly lines. Assembly-line

Above: People used kerosene for lighting throughout the nineteenth century.

Above: Model Ts come down the assembly line at the Ford Motor Company plant in Highland Park, Michigan, in 1914. The low cost of the Model T made it affordable for many people.

manufacturing boosted production and made cars affordable for ordinary people. The Ford Model T was by far the most successful of early cars. The Ford Motor Company had sold more than fifteen million Model Ts by the end of the 1920s.

Huge oil companies formed to supply gasoline for all these vehicles. Giants like Standard Oil, founded by John D. Rockefeller, made vast fortunes by drilling for oil in the United States, refining it, and selling petroleum products—especially gasoline. Rockefeller's stock in Standard Oil and other companies made him the first U.S. billionaire and the richest person in the world. According to many sources, he was the richest person who has ever lived. History remembers Rockefeller and other oil tycoons as captains of industry (recognizing their contributions to society) or as robber barons (suggesting they used unfair business practices to make massive profits).

No matter how one views Rockefeller and his peers, one fact is certain. They forever changed the world economy. Oil became a crucial commodity. Industrialized nations simply could not do without it.

U.S. oil demand soon outstripped U.S. production capacity. As a result, U.S. oil companies became increasingly dependent on foreign sources of oil. The Middle East, which had vast oil reserves, was willing to provide them. In 1920 the United States extracted and imported about sixty million barrels of foreign oil—most of it from the Middle East. A few decades later, annual U.S. oil imports had tripled. And imports kept growing.

THE NUCLEAR AGE

During the mid-1900s, scientists came up with a new and fearsome way to generate power. They tapped into the energy of the atom itself.

The nucleus (center) of an atom consists of protons and neutrons (particles with positive and neutral electrical charges, respectively). The energy that holds the nucleus together is nuclear energy. People can release this energy by combining or splitting atomic nuclei.

Italian physicist Enrico Fermi conducted the first successful experiment with splitting atoms in 1934. From then on, nuclear power offered the world both promise and peril.

Above: Enrico Fermi was the first person to split atoms. This photograph is from the 1940s.

The United States led the way in nuclear experimentation. Fermi and other leading scientists emigrated (moved) from Europe to the United States in the late 1930s to escape political instability. The United States put these scientists to work in the top-secret Manhattan Project. This project's main goal was to study nuclear power and turn it into a weapon. As World War II (1939–1945) unfolded, nations on both sides of the conflict (the Allied and the Axis powers) rushed to develop a nuclear bomb.

The Manhattan Project was a success. It produced the first successful nuclear reactors (energy-producing facilities). It also created facilities to enrich uranium (a naturally radioactive metal) to make it more

Below: Scientists on the Manhattan Project, including Robert Oppenheimer (in white hat), inspect the detonation site of the first atomic bomb in July 1945.

radioactive. (A radioactive substance spontaneously releases energy while gradually breaking down.) Enriched uranium is a fuel used to sustain nuclear reactions and to power nuclear weapons.

By 1945 the United States and the other Allies were entrenched in a bloody campaign against Japan, a member of the Axis powers. The other Axis powers had surrendered, ending the war in Europe. But the war raged on in Asia. Japan refused to surrender.

So in summer 1945, U.S. leaders faced the prospect of invading Japan. The invasion would cost hundreds of thousands of lives and could drag on for years.

Instead of invading, U.S. president Harry Truman tried to force Japan's surrender with nuclear weapons developed by the Manhattan Project. These bombs were more powerful than any weapon in human history. Dropping them on Japan would kill thousands of civilians. The Allies issued an ultimatum, or final demand, to Japan. They

threatened to utterly destroy Japan if it wouldn't surrender.

Japan ignored the ultimatum. Truman and the U.S. military went ahead with their plan. They dropped nuclear bombs on the Japanese cities of Hiroshima and Nagasaki on August 6 and August 9, respectively. The bombs caused massive damage, killed more than two hundred thousand people, and released deadly radiation into the atmosphere above Japan. Japan's emperor surrendered.

World War II was over, and nuclear technology had ended it. But as soon as one threat disappeared, another took its place. After World War II, the United States and the Soviet Union began a nuclear arms race. (The Soviet Union was a union of fifteen republics, including modern Russia, that existed from the early 1920s to the early 1990s.) The two nations had sharply contrasting political systems. Each feared the possible expansion of the other.

The political standoff was called the Cold War (1945–1991). The rival nations built huge arsenals of nuclear weapons. Neither side dared to use the weapons, since the enemy would surely retaliate. The resulting nuclear war would cause worldwide destruction, which nobody wanted. To many people, the term *nuclear* began to mean "deadly and irresponsible."

The quest to develop nuclear energy technology carried on, however. In 1951 an experimental nuclear reactor in Idaho became the first to produce electricity. Three years later, the Soviet Union had a fully functioning nuclear plant providing electricity to its power grid (power transmission network). For good or bad, nuclear power and its risks were here to stay.

THE ENERGY CRISIS

Despite advances in nuclear technology, oil remained the industrial world's most important source of energy. The United States grew more and more dependent on foreign oil through the mid-1900s. As long as other countries kept supplying oil to the United States, that dependence was not a big problem. But in the 1970s, the oil stopped flowing.

The Arab nations of the Middle East were by far the world's biggest oil suppliers. But these nations disagreed with many U.S. policies. They especially

Below: At Idaho's experimental nuclear reactor in 1951, atomic energy lights a string of lightbulbs.

disliked the U.S. alliance with Israel—a Jewish nation frequently at odds with the Arab world.

U.S.-Arab friction came to a head in 1973, when the United States decided to supply Israel's military during the Yom Kippur War. In this three-week war, Israel fought an alliance of Arab nations led by Egypt and Syria. In response to the U.S. decision, the Organization of Arab Petroleum Exporting Countries (OAPEC) declared an oil embargo (reduction or halt in trade) against the United States. OAPEC nations controlled the vast majority of the world's oil reserves. The OAPEC nations immediately increased oil prices by 70 percent. In addition, they vowed to reduce oil production 5 percent per month.

The embargo caused a rush on oil, which in turn caused skyrocketing oil prices. Gasoline prices soared along with oil prices. Shortages led to hoarding and long lines at gas stations.

Suddenly, U.S. policy makers had to think hard about energy. In December 1973, government officials asked Americans to save energy by not turning on Christmas lights. Oregon outlawed the lights. President

Above: Gas stations across the United States ran out of gasoline during the 1973 oil embargo. Those with gas had long lines.

> " **Let this be our national goal: At the end of this decade, in the year 1980, the United States will not be dependent on any other country for the energy we need to provide our jobs, to heat our homes, and to keep our transportation moving.** "

—**U.S. PRESIDENT RICHARD NIXON,** 1974

Richard Nixon asked gas stations not to sell gasoline from Saturday night through Sunday. Most stations complied. Still, the crisis worsened. By February 1974, about 20 percent of all U.S. gas stations had no gasoline to sell.

The embargo ended in March 1974. But U.S. energy policy had changed forever. Ideas like energy conservation, renewable energy, and energy independence gained momentum. The importance of such ideas grew five years later, during a second energy crisis. The 1979 crisis followed political instability in the oil-producing nation of Iran.

A MOVE TOWARD ALTERNATIVES

The oil shortages of the 1970s forced the United States to start developing alternative energy sources. Nuclear power quickly grew more important. Dozens of reactors sprang up around the United States. Nuclear power had loud critics, however. They said nuclear power was unsafe. Critics supported this claim by pointing to a string of accidents at nuclear power plants, including a close call at Three Mile Island in Pennsylvania (1979) and a deadly disaster at Chernobyl in the Soviet Union (1986).

Other energy technologies developed slowly in the United

States. Solar power enjoyed a brief surge in the late 1970s and early 1980s. But as oil prices dropped and stabilized, the push for solar power quickly diminished. Wind farms (large groups of electricity-generating wind turbines) popped up in California and the Great Plains, but the wind farms were small. They played only a bit part in energy production.

The United States turned to coal to meet its ever-growing energy needs. It made perfect sense. The United States had vast reserves of coal. It was easy to mine and use. Oil remained the primary fuel for cars and trucks. But more and more electricity came from burning coal. Americans generally ignored the pollution problems coal created.

Below: Three Mile Island in Pennsylvania is a nuclear power plant famous for having the worst accident in U.S. nuclear power history. After the 1979 accident, one reactor closed permanently. One reactor at the plant is still in operation.

Off the grid or on, solar and wind power gain

From the Pages of
USA TODAY

Amid soaring electricity prices, the renewable energy industry is increasingly being driven by families who choose to be off the grid for environmental or political reasons and by a much faster-rising number of Americans adding solar and wind systems to grid-connected houses. Such equipment used to be bought almost exclusively by off-the-gridders in remote rural reaches who couldn't afford fees of $30,000 or more to tie in to electric lines.

Now, in 27 states, homeowners on the grid can get state rebates or tax breaks that subsidize up to 50 percent or more of the cost of clean energy systems. They then sell the electricity they generate, but don't use themselves, to utilities, offsetting the cost of the power they draw from the grid as they spin their meters backward and drive their electric bills toward zero.

Seventeen states, and some power companies themselves, now offer utility customers rebates on the purchase and installation of solar or wind systems, up from three in 2000. Meanwhile, the number of states with "net metering" laws—which permit customers to sell the power they produce to the electric utility at retail rates—has nearly doubled to 36 in the past six years.

Despite a hodgepodge of state laws, the trend points up a budding grass-roots movement to displace at least some of the nation's power generation from pollution-belching plants to small, clean neighborhood nodes. That eases strains on transmission lines. Some 180,000 families live off-grid, a figure that has jumped 33 percent a year for a decade. Yet, thanks to the incentives, another 27,000 grid-connected houses supplement the utility's power with their own energy systems, most of which are solar.

The movement got an added jolt in January when utility customers could start taking advantage of a new $2,000 federal tax credit for solar power system purchases as part of the Energy Policy Act of 2005. After soaring 30 percent a year the past five years, sales of solar, or photovoltaic, systems could ratchet even higher this year.

For decades, dealers in small solar and wind systems depended on the small band of mavericks who moved off the grid to live in the countryside, where land is plentiful and inexpensive. California, Washington, Oregon, Colorado, Vermont and Maine have long been havens, though people live off the grid in almost every state.

Property without utility hook-ups can cost about a third less than a standard lot. These days, a growing number of off-gridders could link up fairly cheaply but prefer to be untethered for myriad reasons, including rising electricity rates, a desire to cut power plant pollution and concerns about blackouts or terrorism.

The Wilmington area, in rural southern Vermont nestled at the foothills of the Green Mountains, is speckled with off-grid homes on back roads where the area's criss-crossing power lines don't reach.

Doucette, a wood carver, and some friends built his 3,200-square-foot [300-square-meter] house [there] four years ago. Doucette figures his green energy system will pay for itself in 20 years. But money was not at the heart of their decision.

"We made a conscious choice not to get on the grid," Doucette says, noting he has long been rankled by the electricity price increases of the local resort town during ski season and by periodic winter blackouts.

Like other off-gridders, Doucette uses his solar panels as his main energy source. [His wind] turbine provides added juice on cloudy days when the wind is swirling.

The power generated by both solar and wind systems is stored in 24 batteries in a bin in the shed. The batteries could last several days in the unlikely event there is neither sun nor wind. A backup propane generator kicks in if the batteries get low.

Like other clean-energy homes, Doucette's two-story, earth-toned house is built for conservation, with energy-efficient refrigerator and dishwasher, low-voltage light bulbs and straw-bale insulation.

For others, living off the grid is a matter of principle. Maynard Kaufman, 77, who lives in a saltbox house on a farm near Bangor, Mich., could have connected to the grid for $10,000. Instead, he spent $30,000 on a solar power system and $12,700 on two wind turbines. Noting he had demonstrated in front of the local nuclear plant, he said, "It was totally a matter of conscience."

—Paul Davidson

> " The Stone Age did not end for lack of stone, and the Oil Age will end long before the world runs out of oil. "

—SAUDI ARABIAN OIL MINISTER AHMED ZAKI YAMANI, 1986

Meanwhile, some people cautioned that fossil fuels were a dead-end energy source. Coal, oil, and natural gas were finite (limited) resources. U.S. oil production peaked in the 1990s, and world reserves couldn't last forever.

In addition, the environmental impact of burning fossil fuels was a growing concern. By the 1990s, terms such as *global warming* entered the vernacular (everyday speech). Some cautioned that the release of carbon dioxide (CO_2) gas into the air from burning fossil fuels was causing a steady rise in average global temperatures. This rise, in turn, was wreaking havoc with the environment.

In 1997 the world took its first small step toward curbing emissions of CO_2 and other greenhouse gases. (Greenhouse gases contribute to global warming.) That year eighty-four countries signed an international agreement called the Kyoto Protocol. The agreement set targets for nations to lower their emissions. But the United States—the

USA TODAY Snapshots®

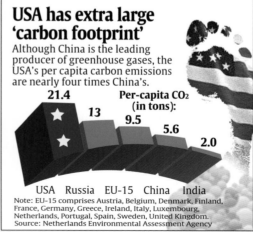

USA has extra large 'carbon footprint'

Although China is the leading producer of greenhouse gases, the USA's per capita carbon emissions are nearly four times China's.

Per-capita CO2 (in tons):

USA	Russia	EU-15	China	India
21.4	13	9.5	5.6	2.0

Note: EU-15 comprises Austria, Belgium, Denmark, Finland, France, Germany, Greece, Ireland, Italy, Luxembourg, Netherlands, Portugal, Spain, Sweden, United Kingdom.
Source: Netherlands Environmental Assessment Agency

By Anne R. Carey and Suzy Parker, USA TODAY, 2008

U.S. Sources of Electricity
(2009)

Coal	45.0%
Natural gas	21.4%
Nuclear	20.8%
Hydropower (electricity generated by moving water)	7.6%
Other sources (including solar and wind)	4.1%
Oil	1.1%

world's biggest CO_2 emitter at the time—refused to ratify the agreement (commit to it). As a result, many people believed it was ineffective.

Wildly fluctuating oil prices in the early twenty-first century increased the drive for clean, renewable, locally generated energy. U.S. dependence

Above: A solar car leads other low-emission vehicles through the streets of Kyoto, Japan, to celebrate the Kyoto Protocol in December 1997.

Treaty harms economy

From the Pages of
USA TODAY
In October, Yale Professor William Nordhaus, a pre-eminent economist, told President Clinton's climate-change symposium that an agreement to return emissions to their 1990 levels by 2010 would be reminiscent of the 1970s energy price shocks and economic stagnation.

In Kyoto, Japan, the United States agreed that we will go well below the 1990 level. Our negotiators activated an economic time bomb that threatens the well-being of American families and workers and the less well-off around the world.

Complying with the terms of the treaty will require Americans to reduce energy consumption by about 30%, a task energy experts know will be impossible without creating economic stagnation.

Moreover, U.S. negotiators in Kyoto declared unilateral economic disarmament and accepted a process that will allow international bureaucrats to dictate our economic future. Theirs is a folly of gargantuan proportions that could haunt Americans for decades to come.

The issue of potential human influence on the climate is legitimate. But the interests of American workers who will lose their jobs, of consumers and farmers who will face higher costs for goods and services, and of businesses that will be disadvantaged in international markets are not served by the agreement.

The fallacy of the treaty is clear on its face. The countries that will be the sources of a majority of greenhouse gases in the future are not required

on foreign oil became a security issue. Many Americans believed the U.S. economy relied too heavily on a resource controlled largely by unfriendly nations. Environmental concern further fueled the demand for green energy.

Scientists strove to develop efficient, renewable energy technology—including solar power, wind power, nuclear to control them, so no matter what actions the United States takes to lower emissions, global emissions will continue rising. Some of those countries now claim they are "entitled" to a share of the American economy as "reparations."

On Monday, I communicated to Vice President Gore that we support efforts to expand President Clinton's voluntary emissions-reduction programs and larger commitments to research and develop new technologies that can be applied worldwide to reduce emissions.

A legally binding treaty that hobbles the U.S. economy cannot be justified. The president should refuse to sign the Kyoto protocol. If he does not, I believe the signs are clear that the Senate will deal a swift denial of ratification.

—William F. O'Keefe, chairman of the Global Climate Coalition, on the editorial page

Above: President Bill Clinton speaks to reporters at John F. Kennedy airport in New York City after returning from Kyoto, Japan.

power, clean coal (less-polluting coal-fired power plants), and more. Automakers focused on improving fuel efficiency and built electric cars and hybrids (cars that run on both gasoline and electricity). The first steps toward a green energy economy were small, but the movement was truly under way.

CHAPTER TWO

Global Warming: Threat or Hype?

THE WILKINS ICE SHELF OFF WEST ANTARCTICA HAS floated on the Southern Ocean for hundreds—possibly thousands—of years. (An ice shelf is a thick, floating platform of ice that forms where a glacier flows off land and into the ocean.) It lies near the Antarctic Peninsula, between tiny Charcot Island and huge Alexander Island. The ice shelf is about the size of Jamaica.

In 2008 the ice shelf began melting. Huge chunks of it were breaking off. Soon only a narrow ice bridge linked the shelf with Charcot Island. Then, on April 5, 2009, the bridge shattered, putting the entire shelf at risk of collapse.

The Wilkins Ice Shelf was not alone. At least eight Antarctic ice shelves had recently shown signs of significant melting. And with polar temperatures steadily rising, the melting was likely to continue. The melting ice could raise the level of the Southern Ocean.

Many scientists blame global warming for the melting of so much Antarctic ice. "There is little doubt

Left: A piece of the Ross Ice Shelf breaks off into the Ross Sea in Antarctica.

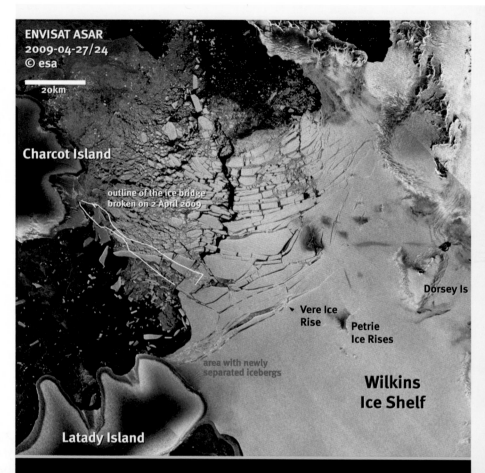

ENVISAT ASAR
2009-04-27/24
© esa

20km

Charcot Island

outline of the ice bridge
broken on 2 April 2009

Dorsey Is

Vere Ice
Rise

Petrie
Ice Rises

area with newly
separated icebergs

**Wilkins
Ice Shelf**

Latady Island

Above: The European Space Agency prepared this photo that shows the major breakups of the Wilkins Ice Shelf.

that these changes are the result of atmospheric warming," said David Vaughan of the British Antarctic Survey.

The partial breakup of the Wilkins Ice Shelf was alarming. But most of the shelf's ice was already floating below the ocean's surface. In addition, the shelf—unlike some ice shelves—was not acting as a dam against a large quantity of glacial ice. So

Global Warming: Threat or Hype?   33

its collapse did not affect global sea levels.

That would not be the case with all ice shelves. Other ice shelves, such as Antarctica's Ross Ice Shelf, hold back massive quantities of glacial ice. The Ross Ice Shelf is the size of France. If a large part of it were to collapse, it could cause ocean levels to rise dramatically. Many scientists believe that if polar temperatures keep rising, large bodies of ice such as the Ross Ice Shelf will surely fail.

WHAT IS GLOBAL WARMING?

Global warming, also known as global climate change, seems to be in the news constantly. What exactly is global warming? What causes it? Can humans stop it?

Earth and its atmosphere work a bit like a greenhouse. In a greenhouse, solar energy passes easily through the panes of glass into the greenhouse. The solar energy warms the objects inside the greenhouse. The warm objects radiate heat.

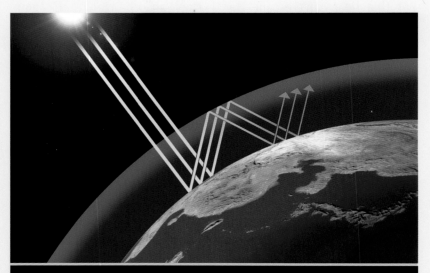

Above: Earth's atmosphere absorbs and reradiates some of the heat released by the planet's sun-warmed surface. This process is called the greenhouse effect.

Runaway Greenhouse Effect

Earth isn't the only planet with a greenhouse effect. Venus has it too.

Venus is closer to the Sun than Earth is. So it's only logical that Venus would be a little hotter than Earth. But Venus isn't just a little hotter. It's a scorching sphere where temperatures soar to 900°F (480°C).

Why is Venus so hot? A thick atmosphere of 96 percent carbon dioxide blankets the planet. The CO_2 traps solar energy and makes Venus a place where life as we know it could never exist.

But that heat can't escape the greenhouse. So the temperature inside the greenhouse rises.

Similarly, solar energy passes easily through Earth's atmosphere to Earth. Snow, ice, and clouds reflect some of this energy directly back out to space. But land, water, trees, buildings, and other objects absorb a great deal of solar energy. As they do so, Earth's surface warms up. The warm surface radiates heat. Some of this heat escapes directly to space. But certain atmospheric gases—greenhouse gases—absorb some of the heat. These gases reradiate the heat they absorb again and again. The overall effect is to trap heat in the atmosphere. This heat-trapping process is called the greenhouse effect. The greenhouse effect keeps our planet warm enough to make life possible here.

The more greenhouse gases Earth's atmosphere contains, the more heat it traps. The atmosphere contains several greenhouse gases. One particularly abundant and important greenhouse gas is carbon dioxide. Our atmosphere is less than 0.04 percent CO_2, but even that little bit plays a big role in setting our planetary thermostat. If the amount of atmospheric CO_2 increases, it traps more heat. That means rising average global surface temperatures—or global warming.

Many scientists agree that atmospheric CO_2 is on the rise and that Earth's average temperature is rising with the CO_2. But where is the increased CO_2 coming from?

Fossil fuels are the answer. For millions of years, countless tons of carbon stayed locked up in coal, oil, and natural gas reserves. When people burn fossil fuels, they release that carbon into the air as carbon dioxide. It's no coincidence that atmospheric CO_2 has been on the rise since people started relying on fossil fuels to generate power.

WHAT'S THE BIG DEAL?

Earth's temperature change seems small—an average rise of only about 1.4°F (0.8°C) over the past one hundred years. What's the big deal if the average global temperature rises a little? Is that really a problem?

According to most climatologists (scientists who study Earth's climate), it is a very big problem. Earth has never seen such a rapid change in such a short period of time. And even small changes can lead to catastrophic chain reactions.

For one thing, global warming isn't occurring evenly around the globe. Certain places, such as the North and South poles, feel the effects more sharply. Polar regions are warming at two or three times the global average rate. This warming is causing the polar ice to melt.

If allowed to continue, melting polar ice could become a huge problem. Polar ice is made up of freshwater. Depending on how much ice melts, the additional freshwater could raise sea levels anywhere from a few inches to many feet. A rise of a few inches is no big deal to people living 1 mile (1.6 kilometer) above sea level in Denver, Colorado. But to someone living in the coastal cities of Miami, Florida; New Orleans, Louisiana; or New York City, a few inches would spell disaster.

China: U.S. should take responsibility on climate

From the Pages of
USA TODAY

Chinese premier Wen Jiabao reminded the world Thursday that China is serious about tackling global warming—but on its own terms.

Speaking at a meeting of the World Economic Forum, Wen said his government is increasing efforts to cut greenhouse gases. He said richer, developed countries, including the United States, should take the lead in reducing emissions tied to global warming based on their higher per capita emissions and longer history of pollution.

The leader's remarks highlight the complex negotiations ahead of a United Nations meeting in December to work out a global agreement on climate change. President Obama is scheduled to visit China in November.

"Climate change is a common challenge confronting mankind," Wen told the forum of businesspeople, academics and officials. "Each and every country, enterprise and individual should assume a due share of responsibility in meeting the challenge."

After years of fast-paced growth, China recently overtook the USA as the world's leading producer of greenhouse gases such as carbon dioxide, which come from burning coal and oil. Both nations remain heavily dependent on coal, and together are responsible for half of the world's carbon dioxide emissions.

The United States has said it is committed to reaching a deal to reduce greenhouse gases at the U.N. meeting in Copenhagen, if other major polluters such as China and India do their part.

"I see the USA and China as crucial to a deal in Copenhagen," said Yvo de Boer, the U.N. official responsible for brokering an agreement.

Sen. Maria Cantwell, D-Wash., said in Shanghai this week that China and the United States should cooperate to develop clean energy and tap job-creating opportunities.

The market for green technology in China could be as large as $1 trillion annually, according to the China Greentech Report 2009, released Thursday in Dalian. The first signs of a "green transformation" are appearing, said Randall Hancock, co-founder of the China Greentech Initiative, a group of 82 companies, organizations and advisers that issued the report.

China is well-placed to move quickly on "green" products, said Weili Dai, co-founder of Marvell, a Silicon Valley-based semi-conductor company with operations in China, and a member of the U.S.-China Green Energy Council. "The Chinese government can mandate things very easily, as it's not exactly a democracy," she says.

China pushes solar and wind power technology, plus nuclear plants, but "we can't get away from

Above: Chinese premier Wen Jiabao speaks at the World Economic Forum on September 10, 2009.

coal," says S. Ming Sung, Asia-Pacific representative for the Clean Air Task Force, a Boston-based advocacy group for clean coal technology. "In the U.S., 50% of power is generated from coal, and in China, it is 75% to 80%. Coal will be with us for decades to come," Sung said.

"The Chinese government will not be pressured by the international community but is realizing the importance of climate change for its own sake," said Wu Changhua, the Greater China director for the Climate Group, a coalition that works for climate change.

De Boer remains optimistic about the upcoming negotiations in Copenhagen. "The issue is whether China is willing to announce its domestic ambitions," he said. "I hope that on the road to Copenhagen, the USA and China can find even more on which to agree."

—Calum MacLeod

What's worse, melting ice triggers a positive feedback loop, or a cycle that feeds itself. Ice reflects a lot of solar energy back into space. When ice melts, the land or water beneath the ice gets exposed. Land and water absorb more heat, which causes more melting and more sea level rise.

A rise in sea level is just one potential complication of global warming. Earth's weather system is delicate. Small temperature changes can lead to drastic swings in local climates. For example, many scientists worry that huge quantities of freshwater melting into the ocean could disrupt deep ocean currents. Deep ocean currents are like conveyer belts, swirling around the continents in a stable pattern. They distribute heat throughout the ocean. They also play a major role in determining weather.

If melting freshwater alters ocean currents, the currents could in turn disrupt normal weather cycles. Places that usually get moderate rain could experience drought or flooding. The timing of seasons may change, and climate zones may shift. Plants and animals unable to adjust to the changes may die out. People may find they can no longer grow the crops they're used to growing. Areas such as the midwestern United States, which provides much of the world's grain and soybeans, could suddenly become unsuitable for growing these crops. Such a change could put billions of people at risk of starvation.

The chain reaction goes on and on. Earth's oceans absorb CO_2 from the atmosphere. The amount of CO_2 dissolved in ocean water is rising alongside atmospheric CO_2. As a result, seawater is slowly becoming more acidic.

Acid destroys shells. Many sea animals have shells. Among these are krill (tiny shrimplike animals) and many of the animals in plankton (a variety of drifting, microscopic sea creatures). Krill and plankton are food for many kinds of fish and some sea mammals. Without their shells, krill and many of the animals in plankton would die. So would the animals that depend on them for survival.

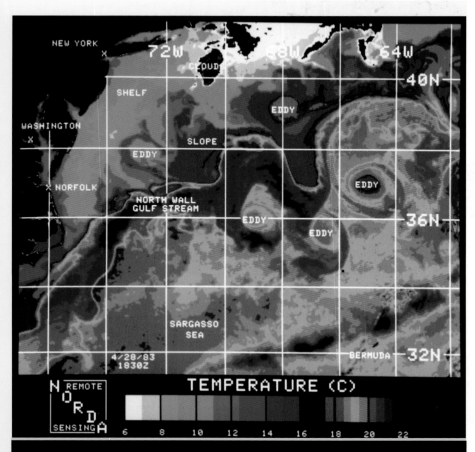

Above: This infrared picture from the 1970s shows the Gulf Stream, a large, warm current in the Atlantic Ocean. Many people worry about the effects of global warming on ocean currents and weather patterns around the world.

People and animals that rely on the oceans for food could find fish in short supply. The scope of such a scenario is hard to imagine.

Nobody knows for sure how things could change as greenhouse gases build up in the atmosphere. The changes might not be as severe as scientists predict. But many argue that the world can't afford to take that chance.

EPA plans to propose rules soon for cuts in car emissions; Agency chief pushes Congress for climate law

From the Pages of USA TODAY

The chief of the Environmental Protection Agency said Monday that the Obama administration is studying how to curb global-warming gases from big industrial polluters such as power plants and factories.

In an appearance before the USA TODAY editorial board, Lisa Jackson also said the agency will soon propose rules to cut greenhouse gas emissions from cars. "We will continue to move stepwise down the path toward regulation of greenhouse gases," assuming that the EPA adopts a preliminary finding that greenhouse gases are a danger to public health, Jackson said.

In May, President Obama said his administration would raise fuel-efficiency standards for cars and light trucks by roughly 40% to cut fuel consumption and reduce greenhouse gas pollution.

There has been no public announcement about how the administration plans to curb greenhouse gases from industrial facilities. Power plants and other industrial plants produce just over half of the nation's greenhouse gases, the EPA says.

Although she is willing to use current law to cut greenhouse gases, Jackson said it

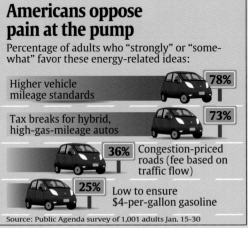

USA TODAY Snapshots®

Americans oppose pain at the pump

Percentage of adults who "strongly" or "somewhat" favor these energy-related ideas:

Higher vehicle mileage standards **78%**

Tax breaks for hybrid, high-gas-mileage autos **73%**

36% Congestion-priced roads (fee based on traffic flow)

25% Low to ensure $4-per-gallon gasoline

Source: Public Agenda survey of 1,001 adults Jan. 15-30

By Anne R. Carey and Alejandro Gonzalez, USA TODAY, 2009

would be better if Congress passed climate legislation. A new law would forestall lawsuits, she said. The House of Representatives passed a climate-change bill in June. The Senate has not yet acted.

A law is also preferable because it could fund clean-energy efforts and other programs that would help fight climate change, said Lou Leonard of the World Wildlife Fund, an environmental group. However, he said, "if the Congress can't move fast enough, then the EPA should act."

Industry groups don't want the EPA to tackle climate in the absence of new legislation, said William Kovacs of the U.S. Chamber of Commerce. The existing law that would be used as the basis of regulations, he said, would require companies to apply for onerous permits if they want to open new facilities.

Regulating industrial sources with current law would be "a job killer and a project killer right at the outset," Kovacs said.

Other issues Jackson addressed:

- The EPA needs to ramp up its work on air pollution, Jackson said. She noted that federal courts have invalidated EPA rules—written during the Bush administration—to control smog and other air pollutants. New rules are a priority, she said.
- Environmental attitudes are changing, she said. Jackson said her sons, ages 13 and 14, were incredulous when they saw a friend's "huge, gas-guzzling" vehicle. "They are going to be very different citizens when it comes to green than my generation," she said.
- A colleague in the administration, Energy Secretary Steven Chu, said Monday on National Public Radio that he'd rather live next to a nuclear plant than a coal-burning plant. Jackson declined to specify which kind of plant she'd rather live next to. "I don't know why he did that," she said, laughing.

—Traci Watson

ARE PEOPLE CAUSING GLOBAL WARMING?

Few scientists deny that global warming is happening. Ample evidence tells a clear story of rising temperatures and CO_2 levels. But what is causing this warming? Are human activities—especially the burning of fossil fuels—to blame? Most scientists say yes, but some question that conclusion.

Some people argue that climate change is a natural occurrence. They claim that humans don't have the power to alter global climate. They say that only natural forces—such as volcanic eruptions, global winds and currents, changes in Earth's tilt on its axis or in Earth's orbit, and variations in solar energy—can influence global climate. They point out that Earth goes through natural cycles of warming and cooling. For example, ten thousand years ago, the planet was deep in the grip of an ice age.

> **What we do over the next decades will affect life on this planet for hundreds of thousands of years, if not millions of years. We are at a critical juncture in Earth history. If we don't do the right thing and there are geologists around 50 million years from now, they'll . . . see remnants of a civilization that developed advanced technology but didn't develop the wisdom to use it wisely.**

—STANFORD UNIVERSITY PROFESSOR KEN CALDEIRA, 2009

> " **I remember as a college student [in 1970] being told it was a certainty that by the year 2000, the world would be starving and out of energy. Such doomsday prophecies grabbed headlines, but have proven to be completely false. . . . Similar pronouncements today about catastrophes due to human-induced climate change sound all too familiar and all too exaggerated to me as someone who actually produces and analyzes climate information.** "
>
> —**JOHN CHRISTY,** PROFESSOR OF ATMOSPHERIC SCIENCE
> AT THE UNIVERSITY OF ALABAMA AT HUNTSVILLE, 2007

Skeptics insist that the recent changes are part of those natural climate cycles. They argue that there's no reason for people to stop burning fossil fuels. And so long as fossil fuels are cheap and plentiful, pushing other forms of energy is a waste of time and money.

Many climatologists scoff at the skeptics' line of thinking. They agree that natural climate fluctuations are real—but they also point out that such fluctuations are gradual. The recent rise in temperature and atmospheric CO_2 is abrupt. Natural processes alone cannot account for this drastic change. It is not, therefore, a natural event. These climatologists argue that human beings are causing the change and bear the responsibility to stop it.

Fixing climate carries big costs; Report: Environment, economy will benefit

From the Pages of
USA TODAY

Global warming's demands on human ingenuity, and pocketbooks, will take center stage Friday in the latest international report on climate change.

The latest International Panel on Climate Change report, "Mitigation of Climate Change," examines fixes—or "mitigation" in climate lingo—to global warming, both technological and economic. The report will underline the environmental and financial benefits of quick action to cut emissions.

But fixes also come with costs explored in the report. If governments, for example, impose fees on carbon dioxide emissions, it would raise the price of electricity for businesses and homeowners alike. For that reason, the USA and China, major users of coal, have objected to calls in the panel's draft report for quick action on just such a move.

In the first of two reports earlier this year, the World Meteorological Organization–sponsored panel, which features thousands of climate scientists reviewing studies, included a best estimate that average surface temperatures will rise roughly 3 to 7 degrees [F, or 1.7 to 3.9°C] this century. In the second report, the panel concluded that environmental impacts of warming were already apparent in migrating species, earlier springtimes and sea-level rise. The summary warned of a future of increased droughts, floods and species extinctions.

A summary of the third and latest report's scientific chapters will be released in Bangkok after review by political representatives of more than 100 nations, including the United States. The key debate in Bangkok will center on a simple chart. The chart shows ways that fast economic moves worldwide, both in technology and in imposing taxes or fees on emissions, would limit global warming. The key goals are keeping this century's average surface temperature rise roughly below 3.6 degrees Fahrenheit [2°C], he adds. That's the point where many dangerous impacts, such as declining grain yields in Africa and the spread of tropical diseases toward the poles, almost certainly loom.

The report evaluates mitigation from a number of angles:

- Technologies ranging from better building design to nuclear power to carbon sequestration [storage], which shunts greenhouse gases from smokestacks into underground rock formations.
- Future emission "scenarios," ranging from a "business as usual" world in which fossil fuel use continues unabated to ones with strict limits on greenhouse gases.
- Economic estimates from combinations of technologies, policies and scenarios.

Money, not science, becomes the point of debate over climate change with the release of the mitigation report, says report co-author Anthony Patt of Boston University. On one side, Patt suggests, some will take the position outlined in February by *Newsweek* pundit Robert Samuelson that significantly changing emissions "would be costly, uncertain and no doubt unpopular." Others will agree with last year's *Stern Review*, an economic review of global warming's implications headed by the United Kingdom's chief economist, which argued that reducing carbon dioxide emissions would lower economic growth modestly this century, while inaction would trigger global recession by 2050 because of the environmental effects of runaway climate change. "I think the report will make plain that a lot of avenues exist" for addressing climate change, Patt says.

No one technology or policy will address climate change by itself, [co-chair of the National Commission on Energy Policy John] Holdren says. "People are starting to notice climates changing, see it in their real lives," he adds. "It's too late to stop global warming. The real question is whether we can prevent catastrophic (man-made) interference with climate."

—Dan Vergano

WHAT CAN WE DO?

Many scientists agree that global warming is real and that people are contributing to it. If that is the case, what can people do to stop and possibly even reverse the effects? Is it too late, or is there still time?

Opinions vary. Most experts agree that climate change is already under way and that no matter what we do, global climate will continue to change in the coming years. Some propose that people accept the change and try to adapt to it. Others believe that mitigation is the proper strategy. Mitigation is the limiting of factors leading to climate change. By reducing the amounts of greenhouse gases released into the atmosphere, people can slow the pace of change. Mitigation is a way of putting the brakes on climate change. Mitigation

Carbon Sequestration

Some people have proposed carbon sequestration (long-term CO_2 storage) as a way to slow climate change. One method for trapping and storing CO_2 is tree planting. Like all plants, trees pull CO_2 from the air and release oxygen, which is not a greenhouse gas. Many kinds of trees can live for hundreds of years. These trees could keep some CO_2 out of the atmosphere for a long time. Tree planting can help, but it only provides a small part of the solution. We just can't plant enough trees to balance the amount of CO_2 we pump into the atmosphere.

Other methods of carbon sequestration depend on human ingenuity. Some people propose capturing the CO_2 released from burning fossil fuels and then pumping and sealing the CO_2 deep underground. Supporters of this method argue that it could trap millions of tons of CO_2. But opponents claim that it would be far too costly and wouldn't help enough to warrant the expense.

won't stop global warming completely, most agree—but it could limit the damage.

The most important part of any plan to curb global warming is reducing greenhouse gas—especially CO_2—emissions into the atmosphere. Every year, the burning of fossil fuels adds 31 billion tons (28 billion metric tons) of CO_2 to the atmosphere, and that amount is growing. One way to reduce emissions is energy conservation. But using less energy isn't enough. As long as people keep burning fossil fuels and dumping CO_2 into the air, the problem of climate change will keep growing. To prevent catastrophic climate change, humans must switch to energy sources that do not release greenhouse gases.

CHAPTER THREE

Nuclear Power: Risk and Reward

BEFORE 1986 FEW PEOPLE OUTSIDE THE SOVIET UNION had heard of Chernobyl. The town, which stood 68 miles (110 km) north of Kiev, Ukraine, boasted a new nuclear power plant. The Chernobyl plant included four nuclear reactors. It produced about 10 percent of Ukraine's electricity. The plant was so successful that officials were building two more reactors there.

On April 25, 1986, plans were under way to test the cooling system of reactor number four at Chernobyl. The test began early in the morning on April 26. But a series of errors by plant officials left the reactor's core with no cooling at all. An uncontrolled nuclear chain reaction started inside the uncooled reactor. (Such a reaction is like the detonation of a nuclear weapon.)

The energy released by the runaway reaction caused a massive explosion. It blew the 2,000-ton (1,814-metric-ton) lid off the reactor. Another explosion followed,

Left: The Chernobyl power plant and the nearby town still stand empty in the early twenty-first century. Chernobyl serves as a warning against nuclear energy for some. Others look past it to the benefits.

throwing huge amounts of deadly radioactive waste into the air.

More than one hundred thousand people from nearby towns and cities evacuated the next day. But for many people, it was too late. Fifty-seven people died almost immediately from exposure to radiation. A cloud of radioactive waste floated over the Soviet Union and spread to neighboring countries. The accident also contaminated the Pripyat River, which flows into the larger Dnieper River. This contamination endangered millions of people. An estimated four thousand cases of cancer in the region are linked to exposure from the accident.

The Chernobyl disaster dominated international headlines for weeks. It was the worst nuclear disaster the world had ever seen. But it wasn't the only one.

Even before the Chernobyl accident, people had been debating the safety of nuclear power. Chernobyl simply heated up the debate. Many people argue that nuclear power just isn't safe. The risk of disaster is too great. And nuclear power's dangerous by-products can create an environmental nightmare, even in plants working perfectly.

Nuclear energy offers a lot of promise. It produces no CO_2 emissions and can produce massive amounts of energy. But do the rewards outweigh the

> " **I think the environmental movement made the mistake of lumping nuclear energy in with nuclear weapons. It's clear to me that no technology will do more than nuclear to reduce our use of fossil fuels.** "
>
> **—PATRICK MOORE,**
> MEMBER OF GREENSPIRIT ENVIRONMENTAL GROUP, 2009

Accident at Three Mile Island

The Three Mile Island nuclear power plant lies in the Susquehanna River near Harrisburg, Pennsylvania. In March 1979, one of the plant's two reactors suffered a cooling malfunction, which caused a partial core meltdown. This destroyed the reactor and released some radioactive gas.

Later, industry officials and government investigators concluded that the accident caused no perceptible public health problems. Some researchers, journalists, and local residents dispute this claim.

This accident was the most serious in U.S. nuclear power history. It drastically slowed nuclear power plant construction in the United States and wrought sweeping changes in engineering, emergency response planning, staff training, radiation protection, and government oversight.

risks? Is nuclear energy "green" or not? This debate has gone on for decades, and it's unlikely to go away anytime soon.

FISSION AND FUSION

Two types of nuclear reactions can produce energy: fusion and fission. Fusion is the combining of two atomic nuclei. Fission is the splitting of one atomic nucleus.

Fusion occurs when two hydrogen atoms combine, or fuse, to form a helium atom. The reaction releases vast amounts of energy. Fusion is the type of reaction that occurs in the core of the sun.

Nuclear fusion is an appealing energy source because the necessary fuel is abundant. Hydrogen is one of the most common elements on Earth. In addition, nuclear fusion produces no radioactive waste. But it's a tricky proposition. Hydrogen nuclei naturally resist (push away from) each other. Only extreme heat and pressure can overcome this natural resistance. These requirements make fusion difficult and expensive to achieve. Scientists haven't yet figured out how to produce fusion energy cheaply and on a large scale.

Fission, on the other hand, is relatively easy to achieve. It uses uranium and plutonium for fuel. Just 1 pound (0.5 kilograms) of enriched uranium can produce as much energy as 1 million gallons (3.8 million liters) of gasoline.

The most common type of nuclear fuel is a variety of uranium called U-235. When engineers bombard a U-235 nucleus with a free neutron, the nucleus quickly captures the neutron. The added neutron makes the atom unstable, and it instantly splits into two lighter atoms. During this split, the atom throws off several neutrons and releases massive amounts of energy.

The neutrons thrown off crash into other U-235 atoms, which then split and release neutrons of their own. This creates a chain reaction. Engineers control the chain reaction within nuclear reactors.

NUCLEAR WASTE

Nuclear fission is relatively easy to achieve, and it can produce massive amounts of energy. Modern fission reactors can produce 1,000 megawatts or more at any given moment. But fission fuels are relatively scarce. And fission has a serious

Above: This container holds enriched uranium. Enriched uranium contains a higher concentration of U-235 than naturally occurring uranium.

Above: The Prairie Island nuclear power plant near Red Wing, Minnesota, supplies about one-fifth of the electricity used by customers of Xcel Energy, the owner of the plant.

drawback. The process produces deadly nuclear waste.

The main type of nuclear waste is spent fuel. This is what's left of U-235 after it's used in nuclear reactors. Spent nuclear fuel contains a nasty mixture of radioactive substances. These substances emit high-energy particles that can destroy living tissue. In particular, exposure to nuclear waste means a swift and painful death to a person or animal.

Nuclear waste stays toxic for thousands of years. People can't make it disappear, so we must store it somewhere. But where?

The first stop for most nuclear waste is a cooling pond. Water slows the fast-moving neutrons that cause nuclear reactions. Water also shields people from the waste's deadly radiation. But the waste can't stay in cooling ponds forever. It needs a long-term disposal site. That could be a secure above-ground facility or a disposal site buried deep underground.

By 2009 more than 120 U.S. sites were storing nuclear waste

Above: This cooling pond contains hundreds of barrels of nuclear waste waiting to be reprocessed. This plant is at the Sellafield facility in Cumbria, England.

in a variety of facilities—none of which are designed to store the waste indefinitely. The U.S. Department of Energy (DOE) had in 1987 proposed a single secure site to store all the nation's nuclear waste—deep below Yucca Mountain in the Nevada desert. The Yucca Mountain site would allow for a combination of natural and artificial barriers to protect people from dangerous radiation. The plan called for sealing the waste in strong, corrosion-resistant containers and then burying the containers far under Yucca Mountain.

USA TODAY Snapshots®

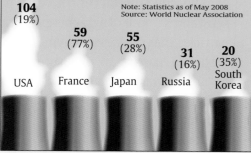

Where nuclear plants are

Nearly 24% of the world's 439 nuclear plants are in the USA. Nations with the most nuclear reactors (and the percentage of that nation's electricity that the reactors produce):

104 (19%)

Note: Statistics as of May 2008
Source: World Nuclear Association

59 (77%)

55 (28%)

31 (16%)

20 (35%)

USA France Japan Russia South Korea

By Anne R. Carey and Julie Snider, USA TODAY, 2008

Work on the site abruptly halted in 2009. The administration of President Barack Obama declared the site unsafe, citing geological instability in the area. The mountain lies near a geological fault (fracture in Earth's crust) that could cause strong earthquakes in the area.

The decision was controversial. Many people supported it—especially Nevadans who did not want to live so close to the world's largest nuclear waste disposal site. "Make no mistake: this represents a significant and lasting victory in our battle to prevent Nevada from becoming the country's toxic wasteland," said Nevada senator Harry Reid of the policy reversal. But others criticized the decision. They pointed out that a failure to consolidate the nation's nuclear waste only increased the danger and expense of storage.

Above: Workers enter the South Tunnel of Yucca Mountain in the early 2000s. Yucca Mountain was the proposed site for a spent nuclear fuel repository. In 2009 the Obama administration stopped work on the site due to possible earthquakes in the area.

Nuclear inches back into energy spotlight

From the Pages of USA TODAY

The nation's nuclear power industry—stuck in a decades-long deep freeze—is thawing. Utilities are poised to build a new generation of nuclear plants thirty years after the Three Mile Island accident, whose anniversary was Saturday, halted new reactor applications. The momentum is being driven by growing public acceptance of relatively clean nuclear energy to combat global warming.

Several companies have taken significant steps that will likely lead to completion of four reactors by 2015 to 2018 and up to eight by 2020. All would be built next to existing nuclear plants.

The steps signal that a nuclear renaissance anticipated for several years is finally taking shape. Seventeen companies have sought U.S. federal approval for 26 reactors since late 2007. All have enhanced safety features.

"The resurgence of nuclear energy is underway," says Steve Kerekes of the Nuclear Energy Institute, an industry trade group. Whether it will yield a flood of new reactors or a trickle will largely depend on the success—or failure—of the initial wave. The industry believes it can avoid the billions in cost overruns and years of delays that marred nuclear construction in the 1970s and 1980s. Licensing has been streamlined. Utilities are seeking firmer costs and schedules. And designs are more detailed.

Still, some hurdles are emerging. Some companies are submitting incomplete applications or seeking design changes at the Nuclear Regulatory Commission (NRC), possibly delaying approval. At least two utilities recently said they're switching to different reactor models because they couldn't receive assurances on costs and the timetable. And since several models are new, problems could emerge as they're built in the USA for the first time. The type of reactor planned for Maryland is being built in Finland, where it's three years behind schedule and $2 billion over budget.

"We're talking about a new generation of technology," says John Reed, CEO of Concentric Energy Advisors. "You have to demonstrate to (lenders) that you can make money with these."

Nuclear plants are hugely expensive, and the credit crisis has all but sealed lenders' wallets. The success of the resurgence also hinges on companies' ability to obtain financing.

Nuclear officials are taking comfort in some encouraging signals from the Obama administration. During his campaign, then-candidate Barack Obama seemed cool to nuclear energy, saying waste storage concerns must be solved before the nation builds new plants. Although the new administration has said Yucca Mountain northwest of Las Vegas is no longer a storage option for the waste, Energy Secretary Steven Chu told Congress this month that nuclear "has to be" part of "our energy future." Waste, he said, can be stored at reactor sites "for decades."

Unlike power plants fueled by coal and even cleaner natural gas, nuclear reactors emit none of the heat-trapping gases blamed for global warming. Obama strongly favors capping global-warming emissions from fossil fuel plants, which would boost nuclear's prospects. Renewable energy is popular but intermittent.

Today, 104 reactors supply 20 percent of the nation's electricity. Just to hold that share, all 26 proposed reactors would have to be completed by 2030. And to meet global-warming goals, 42 reactors should be built in the next two decades, according to the Electric Power Research Institute. Reed says that's possible if the first wave goes well. A new Gallup Poll shows a record 59 percent of Americans favor nuclear energy.

Here's the rub: Nuclear reactor costs have doubled in the past three years to as much as about $8 billion, Moody's Investors Service says. They're twice as expensive as coal-fired plants and triple the cost of natural-gas plants. Reactors also are far more complex, taking up to 10 years to license and build vs. a couple of years for gas-fired plants.

Yet, nuclear plants are far less costly to operate, and the fuel, uranium, is cheaper than coal and natural gas. South Carolina Electric & Gas chose nuclear instead of natural gas to meet some of its power needs because it could produce electricity at retail rates of about 8 cents a kilowatt hour vs. about 10 cents with gas. That's after figuring in subsidies such as production tax credits and before adding potential fees on gas plants for emitting carbon dioxide.

"Nuclear came out to be a better option," says Stephen Byrne, nuclear chief for SCE&G, which plans two reactors near Columbia, S.C. "The cost of natural gas fluctuates pretty wildly."

—Paul Davidson

Nuclear Waste in Space

Some people have suggested disposing of nuclear waste in space. Humans could launch a spacecraft filled with waste and crash it into the sun. If this strategy worked, it would get rid of the waste for good. But it would be expensive. And launching waste in a spacecraft would be incredibly dangerous. Spacecraft don't always make it into space. Equipment failures can cause them to explode in the air or crash to the ground. If a craft full of nuclear waste crashed, toxic radiation would spread for hundreds—maybe thousands—of miles, putting countless people in danger.

The problem of nuclear waste doesn't end with disposal. Even if waste is safely stored, it must then be guarded. Spent nuclear fuel can be used to develop nuclear weapons. Even with crude technology, a terrorist group could turn nuclear waste into a dirty bomb. A dirty bomb is a weapon that combines radioactive material with conventional explosives.

SUMMING UP NUCLEAR

More than any other form of alternative energy, nuclear power comes with strings attached. Used properly, it can

> **If climate change is the problem, nuclear power isn't the solution. It's simply too expensive. Wind-power-hydropower combinations provide the same [base of] power as nuclear plants but at lower cost.**
>
> —KYLE DATTA,
> MANAGING DIRECTOR, ROCKY MOUNTAIN INSTITUTE, 2004

> **The sun doesn't shine at night, and wind power is highly variable. To meet our emissions goals, we're going to have to grasp every arrow in the quiver, and nuclear is one of those arrows.**
>
> —**BURTON RICHTER,**
> WINNER OF THE 1976 NOBEL PRIZE IN PHYSICS, 2009

provide a tremendous source of emission-free energy. But in the wrong hands, nuclear capability could be incredibly dangerous. Even a well-intentioned nuclear power plant improperly maintained could pose an environmental danger. The Chernobyl disaster of 1986, as well as a handful of other less severe nuclear accidents, demonstrates this risk.

Is nuclear energy green? Technically, it falls short of most definitions. While the world's uranium reserves are vast, they are not infinitely renewable. And while nuclear power does not produce polluting emissions, it does produce dangerous nuclear waste. However, many proponents of nuclear energy argue that it is still green—simply because it does not contribute to global warming. In fact, nuclear has the potential to be the biggest single source of CO_2 emission–free power. Therefore, supporters say, nuclear energy is a critical part of any climate change mitigation plan.

Americans seem to be warming to nuclear energy. For decades the technology inspired distrust, but that reaction has been changing in the twenty-first century. A 2001 Gallup Poll showed that only 46 percent of Americans favored nuclear power. By 2009 that number had climbed to 59 percent. This growing acceptance and the fact that nuclear power is a proven technology suggest that nuclear power will be a major part of the United States' energy future.

CHAPTER FOUR

Solar Power: Harnessing the Sun

WHEN PRESIDENT OBAMA VISITED NEVADA'S NELLIS Air Force Base in May 2009, he wasn't there to talk about a new fighter jet or about U.S. military efforts. He was there to call attention to a unique feature of the desert base—its huge electricity-generating solar array. A solar array is a linked collection of solar panels.

The Nellis array covers 140 acres (57 hectares). It contains more than seventy-two thousand solar panels. The panels automatically follow the sun's position through the day, producing up to 315 megawatts of electricity—about 25 percent of the base's total need.

"That's the equivalent of powering about 13,200 homes during the day," Obama told the crowd gathered to hear his speech. "It's a project that took about half a year to complete, created 200 jobs, and will save the U.S. Air Force, which is the largest consumer of energy in the federal government, nearly $1 million a year. It will also reduce harmful carbon pollution by

President Barack Obama *(left)* tours the solar array at Nellis Air Force Base in Las Vegas with base commander Colonel Howard Belote *(center)* and Nevada senator Harry Reid *(right)* in May 2009.

24,000 tons [21,773 metric tons] a year, which is the equivalent of removing 4,000 cars from our roads. Most importantly, this base serves as a shining example of what's possible when we harness the power of clean, renewable energy to build a new, firmer foundation for economic growth."

The array's construction was a partnership between the U.S. Air Force and private industry. The array formally began operation in December 2007. Supporters say it's a bold step toward reducing U.S. dependence on fossil fuels. Detractors, however, point out the array's shortcomings. If a very large array can't produce enough electricity to fully power one medium-size base, how could solar power ever supply an entire metropolitan area?

Skeptics notwithstanding, the Nellis array may be just the beginning. In 2008 the U.S. Army announced plans to build an even larger solar array at Fort Irwin, a major army training

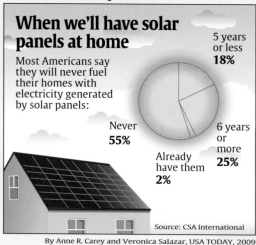

USA TODAY Snapshots®

When we'll have solar panels at home

Most Americans say they will never fuel their homes with electricity generated by solar panels:

5 years or less
18%

Never
55%

6 years or more
25%

Already have them
2%

Source: CSA International

By Anne R. Carey and Veronica Salazar, USA TODAY, 2009

center in California's Mojave Desert. Army officials expect the array to produce 500 megawatts of electricity.

From the government sector to the private sector, solar power is gaining momentum in the United States. Supporters see it as an important energy technology for the future. But can solar become cheap enough and efficient enough to be a big part of the world's energy solution? Only time will tell.

HOW IT WORKS

The sun provides Earth with massive amounts of energy.

The trick with solar energy is collecting and storing it. In the 1860s, French math teacher Augustin Bernard Mouchot developed the first solar-powered steam engine. Ever since then, people have been searching for easy, efficient ways to harness the sun's power. Modern solar technology consists of two main types: photovoltaic and solar thermal.

The photovoltaic cell, or solar cell, is the most common technology people use to harness solar power. A solar cell converts sunlight directly into electricity.

A solar cell is made mainly of materials called semiconductors. The most common semiconductor used in solar cells is the chemical element silicon. The silicon in a solar cell is mixed with traces of other elements.

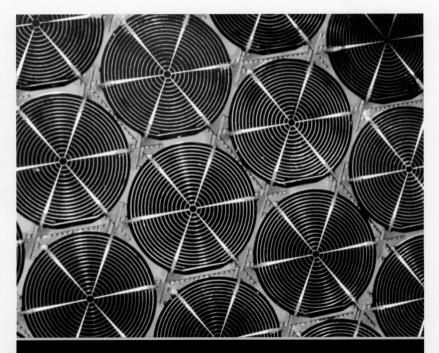

Above: Photovoltaic cells convert sunlight directly into electricity by using a semiconductor to form an electric current.

Companies give folks solar help to go green

From the Pages of
USA TODAY

Companies [are] upending solar's traditional business model by supplying systems to homes and businesses at minimal or no cost, owning and maintaining them, and charging customers for the power they use. The setups, called power purchase agreements (PPA), are among several initiatives that aim to overcome solar's obstacles—high upfront costs and design and maintenance hassles—and deliver systems to millions of customers. "Increasingly, individuals won't have to" buy systems, says Ron Pernick of research firm Clean Edge.

Solar energy emits no global-warming gases, and provides power midday, when demand and electric prices are high. While U.S. solar power has grown at least 45 percent each of the past two years, it makes up less than 1 percent of U.S. power generation, largely because of its cost.

Solar-panel prices are projected to drop 50 percent in a few years. Yet achieving widespread adoption will likely require big buyers that can achieve cost efficiencies, says Travis Bradford, president of research group Prometheus Institute. Among the new models:

Power-purchase agreements. Under these typically 20-year contracts, businesses pay no money upfront. With such favorable terms, PPAs have exploded among companies and government users.

Normally, a big store or factory could spend up to $4 million on a solar system after government incentives. MMA Renewable Ventures, a top PPA provider, shaves system prices 25 percent by snaring high-volume discounts and low interest rates to finance the panels.

To be sure, a business or homeowner could finance a system with a small down payment and monthly payments at or below utility prices. But PPAs offer other advantages. Providers tailor systems to a customer's needs. They navigate a financial maze that includes securing government rebates and tax breaks and figuring depreciation. And they handle upkeep. Customers, meanwhile, have the option to buy the systems at a reduced price after a few years.

To help meet its goal of using 100 percent renewable energy, Wal-Mart last year signed a deal with [power company] SunEdison to install solar systems on 21 Wal-Mart stores and Sam's Clubs in California and Hawaii. By choosing a PPA, Wal-Mart avoided plunking down tens of millions of dollars for panels and having to oversee them. The systems will supply up to 30 percent of its power at a "modest" discount to standard rates, says David Ozment, Wal-Mart head of regulated utilities.

Unlike businesses, homeowners, at least for now, must pay an initial fee of a few thousand dollars or more for their panels because the smaller systems cost more per kilowatt. Still, if power prices rise an expected 5.5 percent a year, [a homeowner] will recoup [a] $6,000 investment in 10 years.

Cities. Several California cities plan to sell bonds to finance solar systems for residents. Berkeley Mayor Tom Bates says the city can get discounts for buying systems in bulk and secure a bond with rates much lower than a resident could obtain through a home-equity loan. An average homeowner who opts into the program would own the system without spending a dime. Finance payments would be $139 a month higher for 20 years—at or below power-bill charges—and rolled into property tax bills.

Utilities. Solar power can help utilities meet state renewable energy mandates. While solar power systems are about 30 percent more expensive than nuclear plants, [utilities] can pare costs by buying systems in large volumes.

What's more, placing units at thousands of homes and businesses lets the utility avoid expensive substation upgrades and insulates customers from outages. Batteries would store solar energy that could be tapped when wholesale power prices spike on hot summer days. Customers likely would get a discount on their electric bill in return for turning their rooftops into mini-power plants.

As more homes and businesses go solar, experts say utilities will take a more active role. Otherwise, they "risk losing their relationships with customers," Bradford says.

—Paul Davidson

When sunlight strikes a solar cell, the semiconductor absorbs some of the solar energy. The energy frees some electrons from the atoms in the semiconductor. The moving electrons create an electric current. Metal contacts at each end of a solar cell allow people to draw off the current as electricity.

Sunlight is made up of a variety of wavelengths, or energy levels. Only some of those wavelengths have just the right amount of energy to create an electric current within a solar cell. The percentage of energy a solar cell captures from the sunlight that hits it is called its efficiency. The most advanced solar cells have an efficiency of more than 30 percent. But most solar cells capture about 20 percent of the energy that strikes them.

People can place solar modules (groups of linked solar cells) in large arrays, on rooftops, in siding on buildings, and in many other locations. Solar panels are

Above: Solar modules can work just about anywhere—including this barn in New Hampshire. But they generate the most energy in sunny climates.

Above: Solar water heaters are simple, small-scale solar devices. The dark surface absorbs the sun's heat and uses it to heat water.

just one type of solar module. Small solar modules can power anything from a cellular phone to a streetlight.

Solar thermal technology is another common way to capture solar energy. A solar thermal system harnesses the heat of sunlight.

There are several different types of solar thermal systems. The type most applicable to large-scale power generation is the heat engine. First, a collection system of lenses or mirrors focuses large amounts of sunlight onto a receiver. A material sealed within the receiver—usually a liquid or a gas—absorbs the sunlight's heat. That heat or the pressure it creates either turns a turbine or makes a set of pistons move up and down. The movement of the turbine or the pistons generates an electrical current.

Other types of solar thermal systems have smaller-scale uses. For example, solar water heaters use sunlight to warm water used for cooking, bathing, and other tasks. Most solar water heaters have dark plates on their surface to soak up the sun's heat. The plates transfer the heat to water stored in an insulated tank. Solar cookers work in a similar way. A solar cooker can be as simple as a glass-covered box with dark sides. The dark sides absorb solar energy, converting it into heat, while the glass top traps the heat inside. The heat bakes food inside the cooker. More complicated solar thermal systems can be used for heating and cooling a building.

Above: Solar cookers, like this Sun Oven, use solar thermal power to heat food.

The solar pond is yet another type of solar thermal system. Solar ponds use very salty water to absorb sunlight. The heat collects in the densest, saltiest water at the bottom of the pond. People draw off the very hot water from the bottom of the pond and use it to generate electricity or for heating.

THE PROS AND CONS OF SOLAR POWER

The sun is a source of plentiful energy for Earth. Each year the sun gives Earth's surface more than ten times as much energy as is stored in all the world's fossil fuel and uranium reserves.

Solar power is also renewable. As long as the sun continues to burn, it will radiate energy. Scientists expect the sun to keep providing a life-sustaining level of energy to Earth for about one billion years.

> **" Sometimes I'm 50 feet [15 m] up on a steep roof and it's so hot the tar is melting onto the bottoms of my sneakers. But I'm excited because I'm helping the environment. "**
>
> **—SPENCER BOCKUS,** EMPLOYEE OF A CALIFORNIA COMPANY
> THAT INSTALLS ROOFTOP SOLAR PANELS

Solar energy is not only abundant and renewable, it is also clean. It releases no chemical pollution into the air, water, or soil. Nor does it add greenhouse gases to the atmosphere.

Solar power sounds like the perfect solution to the world's energy problems. But some people argue that solar power is not all it's cracked up to be.

Solar power doesn't work equally well everywhere. The sun is a reliable source of power in places that get a lot of strong, consistent sunlight, such as Phoenix, Arizona. But places with cloudy climates, such as Seattle, Washington, and places far from the equator, such as Anchorage, Alaska, get far less sunlight. Nighttime poses

Megasolar

A 1999 *Science* magazine article reported that a 100–square-mile (259 sq. km) solar array in the Nevada desert could provide the United States with all the electricity it needs. The cost of building such a massive array would be enormous, however, and transporting the energy efficiently across the country would be all but impossible with existing technology.

Solar Panels in Space?

Some scientists have suggested placing solar panels in space, in high orbit around Earth. Orbiting solar panels would get strong, constant sunlight. The panels could beam their energy back to Earth using microwaves. An orbiting solar array could produce a lot of energy, and several companies have laid out plans for such systems. But cost might prevent space-based solar power from ever becoming a realistic operation for large-scale energy production.

another challenge. Regardless of location, a solar device receives no energy after the sun sets.

For solar power to work around the clock and around the globe, people need a way to store large amounts of energy. But even the best batteries can't store significant amounts of electricity unless they are very large. Many batteries release their energy too slowly to provide large amounts of reliable electricity. In addition, solar batteries are costly to make and have short life spans.

Scientists and engineers are searching for better ways to store solar energy. New types of batteries are one possible solution. New batteries would have to address three problems: size, energy release, and life span.

Solar thermal systems offer perhaps the most promising way to store solar energy. Because these systems turn solar energy into heat, they can continue to produce energy even at night. People can pump heated water or other fluids into insulated tanks and then draw off the hot fluid later and use that heat to generate electricity.

Using daytime solar electricity to make hydrogen fuel could be another solution. People can make hydrogen fuel by passing electricity through water. This process separates the hydrogen and oxygen molecules in each water molecule.

Earth spins on its axis while orbiting the sun. So at any location on Earth, the sun's position in the sky changes through the day and the year. This movement presents another problem for solar power. Solar energy collectors work best when pointed directly at the sun. Fixed collectors, therefore, work well for only a short time. Sun-tracking devices can reposition solar collectors as needed, but these devices add expense.

Expense is, in fact, a big criticism of solar power. Storage batteries and sun-tracking devices aren't the only costly aspects of solar power. The cost of manufacturing and installing solar energy collection devices is high too—for both photovoltaic and solar thermal systems. The systems can produce energy cheaply once they're running, but the startup costs are significant. Because fossil fuels are still abundant and because both nuclear and fossil-fuel power plants are already operating, these energy technologies remain cheaper. Solar power can't yet compete with them.

Below: D. Bruce Osborn, president of Stirling Energy Systems, shows a reporter around a test array. Its dishes turn with the sun and focus sunlight onto heat engines to produce solar thermal power on a large scale.

Chill settles on once-hot solar panel companies

From the Pages of
USA TODAY

Summer may be winding down, but investors holding solar energy stocks are getting one nasty burn. Shares of companies that make solar panels have flamed out this year, missing out on what's been a significant recovery in the stock market.

Market leaders, including First Solar and SunPower, for instance, are down 12% and 30% this year, even as the benchmark Standard & Poor's 500 index is up 13%. And the Market Vectors Solar Energy ETF, which tracks stocks in the industry, is down 6% this year.

Unlike the big drops in other once-hot stock groups, solar's troubles aren't just caused by speculators rushing out. There are some real problems in the industry behind the sell-off of the stocks:

- A glut of solar panels. Makers of solar panels were so sure demand would surge this year, they went into overdrive producing them, says Christine Hersey, analyst at Wedbush Morgan.

   But the flood of supply has swamped demand. Prices of solar modules are in free fall, down about 50% since last year, says Nathaniel Bullard of energy market research firm New Energy Finance. Solar panels now sell for about $2.50 per watt, he says.

- Questions over government subsidies. Thanks to generous programs to encourage green power, European nations have been top buyers of solar modules. However, many are scaling back their subsidies, causing more softness in demand.

   Last year, for instance, Spain put a cap on its solar incentive program, causing the demand from a country that accounted for a big piece of the market to shrink 80%, Bullard says. Of even more concern is Germany, the largest solar consumer in the world, which is mulling a cut to incentives to buyers of solar power, Hersey says. "Since Germany is the largest market, it sets the tone," she says, adding some solar companies get 60% of revenue from Germany. The subsidies have become unpopular because much of the money is going to Chinese, not German, solar companies, she says.

• Challenging environment to borrow money for solar projects. Solar installations require significant upfront costs, and companies and consumers are still having trouble getting such loans, says John Hardy of Broadpoint AmTech. Normally, the decline in solar module prices would be enticing, but unless companies and consumers have the cash, such projects may be pushed off, he says.

There are bright sides to the industry's woes. Consumers can install a home solar system for $10,000 on average, says Bullard. While still pricey, it's half last year's tab.

And investors who pick the companies that survive this shakeout will likely be rewarded. "It's a difficult time for the solar manufacturers, but the ones that come out of this will likely be the world leaders," Bullard says.

—Matt Krantz

■ SOLAR STOCKS SWOON

Several of the leading makers of solar energy equipment are struggling this year, missing out on a strong stock market rally.

Company	Change in 2009
LDK Solar	-31.9%
SunPower	-29.5%
JA Solar	-19.5%
First Solar	-12.0%
Solarfun Power	3.0%

Source: Standard & Poor's Capital IQ

One Million Solar Roofs

In April 2006, California lawmakers passed the state's Million Solar Roofs legislation. The program's goal is to help fund at least one million solar homes in California by 2016. The state set aside more than three billion dollars for rebates to homeowners and business owners who installed solar panels on their roofs. California picks up about half the cost of each installation.

The program was an instant success. California's total number of new solar roof installations in the first nine months of the program almost equaled the state's total number over the previous twenty-six years. Californians clearly want solar power. They just need some help from the state government to make it affordable.

But solar supporters argue that in the long term, solar power will be cheaper than other energy technologies. Fossil fuel prices will probably keep climbing as the world's reserves dwindle. And as more individuals, businesses, and governments invest in solar power, research and development will kick into high gear. Better efficiency and cheaper manufacturing will

> " **If you want to provide one megawatt of electricity, this one megawatt as generated by solar means will be very, very, very costly [in a region where oil and natural gas are abundant and cheap].** "
>
> **—ABDUL MOHSIN,** BP SOLAR, SAUDI ARABIA, 2004

steadily bring down the cost of solar power. It won't be long, many argue, until solar power can provide a large portion of public electricity—especially in sunny areas such as the south-western United States.

Not everyone is excited about the growth of solar power. A proposal to build several solar facilities in California's Mojave Desert met resistance in 2009. Those who stood against the development argued that large solar arrays would destroy the area's natural beauty. They also said that such facilities could harm local tortoise populations.

They "would destroy the entire Mojave Desert ecosystem [community of living things]," said David Myers, executive director of the Wildlands Conservancy. Senator Dianne Feinstein of California introduced legislation to make the land a national monument. That would prevent any future development there.

Others derided objections to Mojave Desert facilities, including California governor Arnold Schwarzenegger. "If we cannot put solar power plants in the Mojave Desert, I don't know where the hell we can put [them]," he said.

The Mojave Desert *(above)* covers much of the southwestern United States, including parts of California.

Renewable energy plan creates rift

From the Pages of
USA TODAY
The morning heat hits triple digits as a whiptail lizard darts below a creosote bush near Route 66. Gazing across the desert valley, power company executives, environmentalists and federal land managers stand beneath a cloudless sky and argue over the landscape.

PG&E project manager Alice Harron says she is "comfortable" with the solar power plant her utility wants to build on government land here. David Myers of the Wildlands Conservancy is not. Renewable energy projects such as this one—which could power 224,000 homes—sound good in theory, he says, but if they tear up pristine vistas, they're not "green."

President Obama wants a "clean-energy economy" that relies on renewable sources such as solar and wind power instead of coal and oil. He wants to put these new utilities on federally owned lands like this stretch of the Mojave Desert, one of the sunniest places on Earth. The administration wants to lead the way by taking advantage of its vast holdings, which account for 20% of all land in the USA, mostly in the West.

That idea is creating a rift among environmentalists, who favor renewable energy but are at odds over where to produce it. Some are willing to compromise with utility companies to build large power plants on remote federal lands to accelerate the transition to clean energy. Purists are dead set against disturbing pristine landscapes.

One purist is Myers, who worries that the government will industrialize the desert with acres of solar mirrors, trampling treasured landscapes. Groups such as the Natural Resources Defense Council (NRDC) counter that large, centralized projects are needed to speed the shift to non-polluting energy. "It's hard, because many of us have fought to protect the very lands" that could be affected, says Johanna Wald of the NRDC.

Interior Secretary Ken Salazar has designated 24 tracts in six Western states as possible solar project sites. There is none on federal lands now.

There are 158 pending solar projects on 1.8 million [0.7 million hectares] acres of public land. If all went through, they could power 29 million homes.

Not all will be approved, Salazar says, because of environmental and other concerns. Still, the White House plans to streamline approval for at least 10 solar plants it hopes will create 50,000 jobs by 2011.

Nearly half the solar proposals are in the Mojave Desert, home to the threatened desert tortoise, Indian petroglyphs and an intact stretch of Route 66, [a] historic highway.

PG&E consultant Scott Galati tells environmentalists that surveys reveal no rare plants or threatened species on a planned solar site. A nearby rail line and access road are proof, he says, the land is hardly pristine.

Myers of the Wildlands Conservancy says an abandoned farm farther from Route 66 would be a better choice. PG&E's Harron says it is privately owned and would be difficult to acquire. The great advantage of government land, she says, is how much of it there is and the relative ease and cost-effectiveness of building projects on public property.

Too easy, says Sen. Dianne Feinstein, D-Calif. In a letter to Salazar last month, she said she was "deeply concerned" about a "bias under which solar developers believe they are more likely to receive a permit to build their projects on pristine public lands than on previously disturbed private lands."

Myers fears taxpayers are subsidizing inappropriately large-scale projects. He'd prefer a focus on rooftop solar panels and other small-scale solutions in urban areas that would reduce the clout of big energy companies.

Wald, the NRDC lawyer, says the government is taking a balanced approach. She spent 35 years battling the oil and gas industry and now is working with them to find appropriate sites for wind and solar plants. She says Myers' approach would take too long. "Even if (some environmentalists) don't like it," she says, large-scale projects "are going to happen."

—Andrea Stone

CHAPTER FIVE

Wind Power: Solution or Nuisance?

IN 2005 MAINE WAS INVESTIGATING WAYS TO PROMOTE green energy. Wind power was at the top of the state's priority list. A proposal to build several wind farms promised to provide up to 40 percent of the state's electricity. That meant 40 percent less pollution and progress toward energy independence—a fantastic scenario, according to many environmental groups.

But others argued that Maine's wind power proposal was far from fantastic. At the center of the controversy was the proposed Redington Wind Farm. This facility would provide about 90 megawatts of power—enough to power about forty thousand homes. But the wind farm would lie within 1 mile (1.6 km) of the Appalachian Trail, in forested land known for its pristine beauty. Opponents argued that the wind farm, as well as the roads needed to support it, would destroy

Left: Open spaces, like this area near the end of the Appalachian Trail in Maine, make the best sites for wind farms. But open spaces are also the most likely to be the focus of preservation efforts.

the area's natural beauty and put wildlife at risk.

The Redington controversy illustrates "a conflict between a desire to move toward clean energy and a desire to protect some of the few remaining wild places," said Pete Didisheim, advocacy director for the Natural Resources Council of Maine. This conflict has raged for years. Opponents have fought hard to block building permits for the wind farm, but many experts believe it is a losing battle.

HOW IT WORKS

People use wind turbines to convert the kinetic energy in wind into electricity. A wind turbine includes three main parts: a rotor, a shaft, and a generator.

The rotor looks like a fan. It is a set of blades attached to a hub. As wind pushes against the blades, they move. This movement makes the hub spin.

The hub is attached to a rod called the shaft. As the hub rotates, so does the shaft. The rotating shaft is attached to an electric generator. The generator contains a set of strong

Above: Wind turbines like these in Wisconsin turn the kinetic energy of the wind into electricity.

magnets and a conductor—usually coils of metal wire. As the shaft spins the magnets inside the generator, they produce an electric current within the conductor wire.

The amount of electricity a wind turbine generates depends on several factors, including the size and weight of the rotor blades as well as wind speed and direction. Most wind turbines include devices that read wind speed and direction and adjust the rotor position to harness the most possible energy.

No matter how well a turbine is built, it cannot produce significant electricity without a stiff wind. Wind speeds are usually faster well above the ground. For this reason, people usually mount turbines on towers at least 100 feet (30 m) tall.

Catching Air

Wind turbine rotor blades have an airfoil shape, like airplane wings. One surface of the blade is flat, while the other is rounded. Air moves over the flat surface faster than it moves over the curved surface. This creates a difference in air pressure on the two sides of the blade. The high pressure on the flat side of the blade helps push it through the air, increasing efficiency.

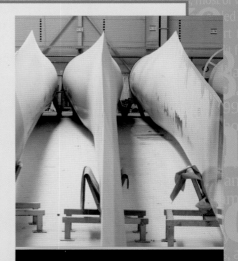

Above: Air moves faster over one side of a turbine blade than the other. This difference makes the blades move.

Vertical-Axis Wind Turbines

When most people think of wind turbines, they picture a horizontal-axis wind turbine (HAWT). A HAWT looks like a fan or a windmill. Its shaft lies within a gearbox that is parallel to the ground. The entire HAWT often sits high atop a tower. But two kinds of wind turbines exist.

The other kind is called a vertical-axis wind turbine (VAWT). A VAWT looks like an eggbeater. Its shaft lies perpendicular to the ground. A VAWT is always aligned to the wind without the need for alignment devices. In addition, a VAWT's generator can lie near the ground, making maintenance easier.

But VAWTs have disadvantages too. They can't start rotating on their own. They need an electrical boost to get started. In addition, VAWTs are less efficient because when the rotor spins, at least one blade is always traveling into the wind. This creates drag, which slows the rotor. Because of these drawbacks, VAWTs are far less common than HAWTs.

Above: These vertical-axis wind turbines are in California. VAWTs come in many different designs.

WIND POWER'S BENEFITS

Wind power has many appealing features. Perhaps most importantly, wind power is renewable. Earth will never run out of wind.

Wind power is also well understood and well developed. Humans have honed the technology for harnessing wind over many centuries.

Wind power is cost effective too. Over time, the cost of wind power is competitive with the cost of nuclear power and fossil fuels.

Another economic benefit of wind power is that it uses a local resource. The money spent developing this resource remains largely in local economies. Wind farms create high-paying technical jobs for local workers.

In addition, wind power is efficient and productive. A single large turbine placed in an area with ample wind can produce almost 2 megawatts of electricity—enough to power about six hundred homes. By hooking together hundreds—or even thousands—of turbines, a wind farm can produce massive amounts of electricity.

Finally, wind power is clean. Wind turbines produce power without creating chemical pollution or emitting greenhouse gases.

> **"Wind farms are an important part of our ongoing efforts to make the United States more energy independent."**
>
> **—U.S. SENATORS BARACK OBAMA AND DICK DURBIN OF ILLINOIS,** 2006

DRAWBACKS OF WIND POWER

Despite all the benefits of wind power, it does have some drawbacks. The variability of wind power and the size, noise, and danger of wind turbines are critics' major complaints.

Exploring new energy strategies

From the Pages of
USA TODAY

George Alcorn is a third-generation Texas oil man. When Alcorn, 51, looks into the future of his business, though, he doesn't see black oil gushing from a well—he sees steam. Alcorn recently revamped his business strategy from traditional oil exploration to using abandoned wells and drilling technology to generate geothermal energy.

The rough-and-tumble image of the Texas oilman may be turning "green." An increasing number of Texas oilmen and companies are swapping oil and gas production for cleaner, renewable-energy strategies.

"We're trying to catch the new wave, not get swamped by it," Alcorn says. "You're going to see more oil companies doing this. There's a great opportunity to make some money here."

As national interest in renewable energy mounts, oil companies are starting to think in renewable terms. President Obama's $800 billion economic stimulus, which contains incentives for renewable projects, has helped push the swing.

The most visible example of the shift has been T. Boone Pickens, the iconic Texas oil tycoon who has been promoting his plan to turn the country toward alternatives such as natural gas, wind and solar energies.

Above: T. Boone Pickens speaks at an energy policy briefing in Washington, D.C., in January 2009.

There are others, including:

- Hunt Oil, a well-known name in Texas oil production, which has a subsidiary researching opportunities in renewable energies.
- Shell Oil, which has teamed with Dallas-based Luminant to build a giant, 3,000-megawatt wind farm in the Texas panhandle.
- Herman Schellstede, a venerable offshore oil explorer from Louisiana who is developing a wind farm off Texas' eastern coast.

The exploration of renewable energy sources by Texas oil executives could have a significant impact on the budding industry, says Michael Webber of the Center for International Energy and Environmental Policy at the University of Texas-Austin. Texas oil companies have the distribution pipelines, deep pockets and subsurface technology needed to quickly ramp up the country's renewable energy supplies, he says.

"These people 60 years ago would go out looking for oil and just find it," Webber says. "That attitude still exists and now they're trying to build wind farms and solar power plants and geothermal fields. It could really change things in this country."

Texas has been the epicenter of the country's oil and gas production since oil first bubbled up in 1901. Today, even Texas lawmakers are ready-ing for a seismic switch from fossil fuels to renewable energy production.

There are currently more than 30 bills related to renewable energy, including 18 solar power bills, in the Texas Legislature that would give incentives to renewable projects. According to state benchmarks, by 2020, Texas should be getting 20% of its energy from renewable sources—leading the nation and much of the world.

Schellstede says he has nearly raised the $311 million needed to install 62 wind turbines on offshore platforms about 7 miles off Galveston's coast. His plan is to install around 900 turbines along the eastern seaboard of Texas at a cost of about $4.6 billion, using existing offshore oil platforms and pipelines.

The transition from oil and gas exploration to wind turbines was an easy one, because much of the oil in the Gulf of Mexico has been tapped, he says. His one regret: not doing it sooner. "We're about 15 years behind," he said.

—Rick Jervis

Like solar power, wind power depends on weather conditions. No wind means no electricity. Even light winds may not be enough to generate significant electricity. Because wind power is variable, other power sources must supplement it. Some experts suggest that even with massive development, wind power will never meet more than 10 percent of U.S. energy needs.

Generating large amounts of electricity requires vast wind farms. These farms must be relatively close to the cities and towns they serve, because transmitting electricity over long distances is difficult and costly. Many people like the idea of using wind power, but few want to live near a wind farm. One turbine might make for an interesting view, but large fields of them get mixed reviews.

Wind farms can be terribly noisy. The turbines produce no physical pollution, but many consider their constant hum to be noise pollution. Noise pollution is more than just a

> " It has been a miserable, horrible experience. [The wind turbines] are 440 meters [1,444 feet] away, but if I step outside and they are not generating I know immediately because I can [finally] hear the silence. They grind you down. You can't get away from them. They make you very depressed. The chomp and swoosh of the blades creates a noise that beggars [defies] belief. "
>
> **—MARK TAPLIN,**
> WHO LIVES NEAR A WIND FARM IN WALES, 2004

nuisance, argue some doctors. It can cause serious health problems, such as migraine headaches, sleep disorders, anxiety, and depression. "There is a public perception that wind power is 'green' and has no detrimental effect on the environment," said Bridget Osborne, a doctor who researched the effects of wind turbine noise on people living near wind farms. "However, these turbines make . . . noises that can be . . . damaging."

People are building more offshore wind farms to minimize the visual and aural drawbacks of wind power. As a bonus, offshore wind farms often receive stronger, more consistent winds than land farms do.

The criticisms of wind power don't end with its impact on humans. Wind farms can be hazardous to wildlife—especially to flying animals such as birds and bats. High death tolls among birds and bats can upset the balance of nature. North American bats, for example, eat huge amounts of insects—especially mosquitoes. When bat populations plummet, insects flourish.

Below: Offshore wind farms are sprouting up as more people complain about the noise from turbines.

Neighbors at odds over noise from wind turbines

From the Pages of
USA TODAY

Not long after the wind turbines began to spin in March near Gerry Meyer's home, his son Robert, 13, and wife, Cheryl, complained of headaches. They have trouble sleeping, and Cheryl Meyer, 55, sometimes feels a fluttering in her chest. Gerry is sometimes nauseated and hears crackling.

The culprit, they say, is the whooshing sound from the five industrial wind turbines near the 6-acre [2.4-hectare] spread where they have lived for 37 years. "I don't think anyone should have to put up with this," says Gerry Meyer, who compares the sound to a helicopter or a jet taking off.

As more turbines are built, the noise they create is stirring debate. Industry groups such as the American Wind Energy Association say there's no proof they make people sick, but complaints of nausea, insomnia and other problems have surfaced near wind farms across the USA.

Nina Pierpont, a pediatrician in Malone, N.Y., calls the ailments Wind Turbine Syndrome and is writing a book on them. In the preface, she says the syndrome "is an industrial plague. It is man-made and easily fixed. Proper setbacks are the best cure."

Laurie Jodziewicz, siting manager for the American Wind Energy Association, says there are almost 15,000 wind turbines in the USA, and most people live near them "without incident. . . . We would have heard if this was a widespread issue."

One of the nation's first nuisance lawsuits against a wind farm ended with rulings in 2006 in favor of the company that developed it. Objections to wind farms continue to be raised:

- Pierpont's website includes reports of illness from Union, Ore.; Mars Hill, Maine; Saginaw, Texas; King City, Mo.; and elsewhere. Wendy Todd, who lives 2,500 feet [760 m] from a turbine in Mars Hill, says she suffers sleep deprivation, and her neighbors have headaches and dizziness.
- British physician Amanda Harry said in a 2007 study that people living near turbines can experience anxiety, depression, and vertigo.

- Mariana Alves-Pereira, a Portuguese acoustical engineer, said in a 2007 study that turbines can cause vibroacoustic disease, which can lead to strokes and epilepsy.

A 2008 study funded by the European Union, however, found that the sound annoys many people, but it doesn't affect health "except for the interruption of sleep."

Some of Meyer's neighbors don't understand the fuss. People who say the noise makes them ill are exaggerating, says Rudy Jaeger, 67, who has a turbine on his farm. "It's no worse than traffic driving by."

The American Wind Energy Association would like to see "a credible, third-party" scientific study, Jodziewicz says. Setbacks are settled between developers and communities, and there's no industry standard, she says.

Susan Dennison, spokeswoman for Invenergy, the Chicago company that built the 86-turbine wind farm here, says it hasn't received any complaints about health problems in the area. Eric Rosenbloom of National Wind Watch, an information clearinghouse, says noise and health concerns are the top issues in communities considering them. The group recommends 1-mile [1.6 km] setbacks from homes. Rick James, an acoustical engineer from Okemos, Mich., suggests keeping turbines 1.25 miles [2 km] from homes.

That makes sense to Larry Wunch, a firefighter who lives a few miles from the Meyers. Turbines encircle his property, and when the wind tops 15 mph [24 km per hour], he says, they "just scream." The closest is 1,100 feet [335 m] from his house.

Wunch says he and his wife, Sharon, "have lost sleep and are irritated." He worries his home's value has declined and says the wind farm has created tension between opponents and those who have them on their property in exchange for annual payments that Dennison says are about $5,000 a year. "It's really turned our township upside down," Wunch says. "If it's affecting your health," Meyer says, "it's hard to ignore."

—Judy Keen

A West Virginia wind farm was responsible for more than two thousand bat deaths in one year. One of the earliest large U.S. wind farms, Altamont Pass Wind Farm in California, is notorious for killing birds. Each year about forty-seven hundred birds die in collisions with the five thousand-plus turbines at Altamont Pass. The annual casualties include more than one thousand raptors (birds of prey), such as golden eagles.

Several environmental protection groups have sued Altamont Pass Wind Farm over the bird deaths.

"Altamont has become a death zone for eagles and other magnificent and imperiled birds of prey," said Jeff Miller, a spokesman for the Center for Biological Diversity, one of the groups that sued the facility. "Birds come into the pass to hunt and get chopped up by the blades."

Above: Jeff Miller, a spokesman for the Center for Biological Diversity, walks outside the Altamont Pass Wind Farm in California. Miller argues that the benefits of the wind farm do not make up for the threats to animal species, especially birds, in the area.

Partly as a result of legal action, Altamont Pass officials have taken measures to protect birds. For example, they have relocated some of the deadliest turbines—those that stood in areas with especially heavy bird traffic. But because of the area's dense bird population, only a shutdown would completely eliminate the problem.

Bird deaths are not unique to Altamont Pass. The problem is so common that many wind power companies check bird migration patterns in local areas before setting up wind farms. Other solutions are higher towers and slower-spinning rotors.

Proponents of wind power argue that in the big picture, the wildlife death toll from wind turbines is not high.

They say that communications towers and high-rise buildings are equally or more dangerous to birds and bats.

Despite the drawbacks of wind power, the industry is growing rapidly. The technology people use to harness the wind and transmit its energy is steadily improving. As a result, wind energy is likely to become cheaper and cheaper relative to fossil fuels and nuclear power.

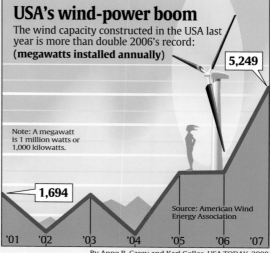

USA TODAY Snapshots®

USA's wind-power boom

The wind capacity constructed in the USA last year is more than double 2006's record: **(megawatts installed annually)**

5,249

Note: A megawatt is 1 million watts or 1,000 kilowatts.

1,694

'01 '02 '03 '04 '05 '06 '07

Source: American Wind Energy Association

By Anne R. Carey and Karl Gelles, USA TODAY, 2008

CHAPTER SIX

Biomass and Biofuel: Growing Energy

THE STREETS OF HAITI, A SMALL ISLAND COUNTRY IN the Caribbean Sea, were a rough place in spring 2008. Haiti is one of the poorest nations in the world. In 2008 many Haitians were having an even harder time than usual putting food on their tables.

Haiti relies heavily on imports to feed its people. Food prices soared worldwide in 2007 and 2008. The bare basics soon cost more than most Haitians could afford. Thousands of hungry, angry people poured into the streets to protest government policies that had contributed to this problem.

The protests erupted into riots, overwhelming the nation's police forces. Haitians stormed the president's palace, demanding his resignation. United Nations (UN) peacekeeping troops had to help restore order.

Left: Angry Haitians take to the streets in April 2008 to protest high food prices. Some people blame high food prices at least partially on the rise of corn ethanol.

Haiti was not alone in its plight. Soaring food prices devastated poor people around the globe. Riots and protests—from Morocco to Bangladesh, from Mexico to Egypt—echoed the unrest in Haiti. Some people blamed their governments. Others blamed rising oil prices, saying that food prices reflected the high cost of shipping.

Other protesters had a different complaint. Some nations, including the United States and Brazil, were using food crops such as corn and sugarcane to produce a fuel called ethanol. Mixed with gasoline, ethanol helps power vehicles. According to one estimate, about 33 percent of the 2008 U.S. corn harvest went to ethanol production. That corn was unavailable to feed the world's people. Because less corn was available to the people who needed it, demand for corn grew. Food prices rose as a direct result.

"While many are worrying about filling their gas tanks, many others around the world are struggling to fill their stomachs, and it is getting more and more difficult every day," said World Bank president Robert Zoellick. (The World Bank is a UN agency.)

Below: Corn ethanol plants popped up across the Midwest in the first decade of the twenty-first century. Some people are concerned that the use of corn for ethanol takes food away from hungry people around the world.

Above: This biomass plant burns rice chaff to generate electricity with a steam generator. Burning the rice chaff releases CO_2 into the atmosphere, but only CO_2 that the rice plants absorbed in the first place.

WHAT IS BIOMASS?

Biomass is any living or recently living organic matter that can burn. Biomass includes both plant and animal material. When plants or animals are alive, they take in energy from sunlight or food. They store some of this energy in chemical form inside their bodies or deposit it on the ground as waste. Burning biomass converts its chemical energy into heat. People can use this heat to power an electrical generator.

Burning biomass does release carbon dioxide into the air. But many people consider biomass a green fuel because it releases freely flowing CO_2. Burning biomass from a plant crop releases the same amount of CO_2 the crop took out of the atmosphere as it grew. Burning biomass introduces no new carbon to the atmosphere. By contrast, burning fossil fuels releases carbon that has been out of the atmosphere for millions of years.

Start-ups put farm debris to use as fuel

From the Pages of
USA TODAY

Want to see what you'll be pumping into your car in a few years? Come visit a scruffy patch of land here in sugarcane country, where 15-foot-high [4.6 m] piles of what looks like hay stretch three blocks alongside a gleaming, silver-and-yellow jumble of pipes, tanks and girders.

The hay, actually crushed sugarcane stalks, is feedstock for the first cellulosic ethanol demonstration plant in the USA. The biorefinery cranked up this week and, according to its backers, kicks off a new era of clean transportation fuels that won't compete with the food supply. Corn-based ethanol, by contrast, has been blamed for driving up food prices and doing little to reduce the global warming gases emitted by petroleum-fueled vehicles.

Cellulosic ethanol is made from plant waste—such as wood chips, corn cobs and stalks, wheat straw and sugarcane bagasse (stems and leaves)—or municipal solid waste. Simply put, the nation will soon be running its cars, at least partly, on debris.

The plant will produce 1.4 million gallons [5.3 million liters] of ethanol a year, a fraction of a typical 60 million-gallon-a-year [227-million-liter] corn ethanol plant but far more than the output of the handful of tiny cellulosic pilot plants in the U.S. About a dozen cellulosic demonstration plants and six larger commercial facilities are scheduled to start up by 2012.

Range Fuels expects to complete the first commercial plant in Soperton, Ga., late this year. The $120 million facility will churn out 10 million gallons [38 million liters] of ethanol a year.

That cellulosic ethanol is this close to commercial production marks a dramatic leap forward. Development in recent decades has been stymied by high costs and difficulty transferring technology that works well in the lab to mass production. Plus, every time oil prices tumbled, research funding evaporated. Driving the renewed interest is growing concern about global warming and a belief that Congress eventually will limit carbon dioxide emissions from petroleum-fueled vehicles.

Venture-capital firms have poured $682 million into cellulosic start-ups since 2006, up from $20 million the previous two years. And the Department of Energy has provided nearly $850 million for research and development.

Producers still face hurdles, including a credit crisis that's delaying several commercial plants. But in 2007, President Bush signed a bill mandating that biofuels make up 36 billion gallons [136 billion liters], or 16 percent, of motor fuel by 2022, with 16 billion gallons [60 billion liters] coming from cellulosic ethanol. Corn ethanol consumption, which totaled 9 billion gallons [34 billion liters], or 7 percent of the gasoline market, last year, is capped at 15 billion gallons [57 billion liters].

A big advantage for cellulosic fuel is that refineries can be tailored to a region's leading crop, reducing delivery costs: wheat straw and corn residue in the Midwest; sugarcane in the South; and wood in the Pacific Northwest and Southeast. Corn ethanol refineries are largely confined to the Midwest.

Another selling point is that cellulosic ethanol can cut greenhouse gas emissions by 86 percent compared with gasoline, while grain ethanol trims emissions just 20 percent, DOE says. That's because diverting corn to fuel means razing forests or plowing grasslands to plant substitute corn crops, according to the Natural Resources Defense Council. That releases carbon dioxide into the air.

How much cellulosic ethanol will motorists actually use? Most U.S. gas pumps now contain 10 percent ethanol blends, and the government is testing blends up to 20 percent. In two decades, more flex-fuel cars that can accept blends of up to 85 percent ethanol are expected to be on the road. By then, cellulosic ethanol realistically could replace a quarter of the nation's gasoline—which would dramatically reduce both oil prices and global warming emissions.

—Paul Davidson

Biomass is a very broad resource. Wood from trees—especially sawmill and paper mill waste—is a very common type of biomass. People often burn yard clippings, wood chips, and other organic trash for energy too. Animal droppings, such as those from cattle, make a great heating source. Some wastewater plants generate electricity from the waste they filter out of water. Biomass also includes plant and animal matter processed into fuel before burning.

WHAT IS BIOFUEL?

Processed biomass is called biofuel. Several different kinds of biofuels exist. Among them are ethanol, biodiesel, biogas, and syngas.

The most common biofuel is ethyl alcohol, or ethanol. Any plant with enough sugars, starches, or cellulose (a fibrous substance) can be made into ethanol. Sugarcane and sugar beets are common ethanol sources because of their high sugar content. Corn is full of starches, which convert easily

Above: Sugar beets are common ethanol sources because of their high sugar content. They are also one of the principle sources of sugar in the world.

Fuel from Weeds

Researchers are looking into the seedpods from the *Jatropha* tree as a source of fuel. Unlike corn, the *Jatropha* does not need premium farmland to grow. It grows like a weed, thriving even in poor soil. The oily, inedible seeds are ideal for biodiesel production, and they don't divert resources away from food production.

Above: An employee harvests *Jatropha* fruit in the Ivory Coast. The fruit contains inedible seeds that are useful for biodiesel production.

into ethanol. And most prairie grasses consist mainly of cellulose, making them a good option too.

To produce ethanol, people use machines to grind up the plant matter and chemically convert starches and cellulose into sugars. Then more machines extract the sugars from the plant matter. Next, tiny organisms called microbes feed on the sugars. These microbes produce chemicals as they feed. One of these chemicals is ethanol. Ethanol is a clean-burning fuel. Combined with gasoline, ethanol powers vehicle engines.

Above: This gas station pump sells E10, E85, and biodiesel. All three are biofuels. E10 can be used in a regular gasoline engine and biodiesel in a regular diesel engine, but E85 works only in flex-fuel engines.

Ethanol-based fuel comes in several forms. The most common type is E10, a blend of 90 percent unleaded gasoline and 10 percent ethanol. This blend of fuel is widely available. Almost any car or small truck engine can burn it. Other fuel blends feature a much higher percentage of ethanol. E85 is a fuel that has 85 percent ethanol and 15 percent gasoline. Only specially adapted engines can burn E85. Vehicles with such engines are called flexible-fuel (flex-fuel) vehicles. Because fewer cars can burn it, E85 is less available.

Biodiesel is another form of biofuel. Oil or fat is the main ingredient in biodiesel. The most commonly used oil in biodiesel is soybean oil. Manufacturers can also make biodiesel from waste vegetable oils, waste animal fats, and from algae grown in sewage. Like ethanol, biodiesel comes in a pure form (B100) and in a blended form (mixed with petroleum-based diesel fuel).

Biogas and syngas could also become important biofuels. To make biogas, animal waste goes in a sealed container along with water and microbes. The microbes process, or ferment, the waste. As the waste ferments, it releases a burnable gas mixture containing methane and carbon dioxide. Pipes carry biogas into homes, where it functions in the same way as natural gas. Farmers can use the

waste left over from biogas production as a fertilizer.

Syngas, meanwhile, comes from biomass such as waste agricultural products. Machines heat the biomass until some of its chemical bonds break—a process called gasification. This process releases gases such as carbon monoxide and hydrogen. Tanks collect the gases so people can burn them as fuel.

BENEFITS OF BIOMASS AND BIOFUEL

Burning organic matter for energy has several benefits. Other industries would produce much of this matter even if it weren't needed for energy production. Using sawmill scraps, trash, human and animal waste, and agricultural waste for fuel helps people tackle two problems at once. It reduces the need for disposal while producing energy.

Industrial biomass and biofuel operations create demand for certain crops—especially corn. This demand is a boon to farmers.

USA TODAY Snapshots®

Where E85 fuel is for sale

There are 1,587 places that sell E85 fuel (85% ethanol, 15% gasoline) for the 6.8 million vehicles on the road capable of burning the mixture. States with the most stations:

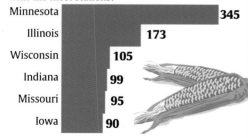

Minnesota	345
Illinois	173
Wisconsin	105
Indiana	99
Missouri	95
Iowa	90

Note: TAll information as of June 23, 2008
Source: National Ethanol Vehicle Coalition (www.e85refueling.com)

By Anne R. Carey and Robert W. Ahrens, USA TODAY, 2008

San Jose knows the way to energy independence; Innovative biogas plant in the works

From the Pages of USA TODAY San Jose is moving closer to becoming the nation's first totally energy independent city. The California city is pushing forward with its "Green Vision" of getting all its electrical power from clean, renewable sources, as well as diverting 100% of its waste from landfills and converting it into energy. In mid-June, the City Council gave the green light to start negotiating plans that could lead to the nation's only organics-to-energy biogas facility.

Renewable biogas, which contains methane, will help power the nation's 10th-largest city, which hopes to reduce its per capita energy use by 50% and get the remaining 50% from renewable sources, says Jennifer Garnett, spokeswoman for San Jose Environmental Services Department. "This project not only demonstrates San Jose's leadership in the production of renewable energy but will help us meet the economic development, zero waste and energy goals of our city's Green Vision," Mayor Chuck Reed said in a statement.

After three years, the Zanker Road Biogas facility would start processing up to 150,000 tons [136,000 metric tons] of organic waste that would otherwise be destined for a landfill to create biogas in addition to high-quality compost that could be used to enrich local soils, says Richard Cristina, president of GreenWaste Recovery. The company is partnering with Zanker Road Resource Management to develop the biogas facility.

The biogas will be produced by the biological breakdown of food waste, as well as the organic share of the municipal solid-waste system, in a process called dry anaerobic fermentation. The dry process, done in the absence of oxygen, is new to the USA, says Michele Young, organics manager of San Jose's Environmental Services Department.

There are similar operations nationwide, but they involve "wet waste," which is easier to recycle than dry waste, Young says. Dry waste is what usually ends up in landfills. The proposed new technology is already in use in 12 facilities in Germany and Italy. Thirteen more are planned for this year, Young says.

The plant will be built on a 40-acre [16 hectare] site near the San Jose/ Santa Clara Water Pollution Control Plant. The energy produced could be used to feed power to the water pollution plant, as well as sold as energy for the utility power grid. The facility will be located between two solid-waste recovery and recycling facilities owned and operated by Zanker Road Resource Management.

The company, together with GreenWaste Recovery, plans to create a "fully integrated waste management system ecopark," Barnett says. Young says she can think of no drawbacks to the project—not even a NIMBY (not in my backyard) argument.

Zanker Road Biogas' plans will be reviewed to determine that they adhere to the California Environmental Quality Act, Young says. The operation's impact on the habitat and neighborhood will be examined to make sure there is no imminent environmental threat.

With any project that might seem too good to be true, there are often pitfalls, says Nathanael Greene, director of renewable energy policy at the Natural Resources Defense Council. "One challenge is dealing with left-overs with concentrated sludge containing pathogens, intact nutrients and antibiotics," Greene says. Poorly handled byproducts could lead to leaks and runoffs that could be devastating to local plant and wildlife, he says. "This is exciting technology," he says. "But we should not assume (it's a) technological panacea."

One of San Jose's Green Vision program goals is to create 25,000 clean tech jobs. About 30 to 40 people would be needed to develop the biogas facility. Once the plant is fully operational, another 50 to 60 positions would need to be filled, Barnett says.

—Danny Chaitin

Corn prices more than doubled from the late 1990s to the late 2000s. Over the same period of time, many midwestern communities built ethanol plants. These plants have provided high-paying jobs and economic growth to rural areas that had been economically depressed. It's no surprise that politicians from corn-producing states such as Nebraska, Iowa, and Minnesota have pushed for government support of ethanol.

Biofuels burn cleaner than gasoline and diesel fuel do. Burning biofuels does release CO_2 into the air, but the emissions are freely flowing carbon. That makes biofuel a valuable green technology, proponents argue.

Politicians have embraced biomass and biofuel production as a major part of a plan for energy independence. In 2005 President George W. Bush signed the Energy Policy Act of 2005. This law required refineries

Above: President George W. Bush signs the Energy Policy Act of 2005. The act was the first major change in energy policy in more than a decade.

to use at least 7.5 billion gallons (28 billion liters) of renewable fuel (mainly ethanol and biodiesel) by 2012. The Energy Independence and Security Act of 2007 extended that requirement to 36 billion gallons (136 billion liters) of renewable fuels by 2022. The required fuels are to be blended into gasoline, diesel, and jet fuel.

DRAWBACKS

Few people can find fault with using farm waste, sewage, or garbage to produce energy. Using waste to create energy is a win-win scenario. Waste-based biomass and biofuel is a relatively easy and cheap energy source, as long as the waste does not need long-distance transport. However, for biomass and biofuel to become a major part of any U.S. energy plan, production will have to use far more than just waste materials. People must grow biological material specifically for energy usage. That's where the debate begins.

Opponents point out that industrial biomass and biofuel operations—especially ethanol and biodiesel ones—create more problems than they solve. The biggest argument against these technologies is that they use resources once dedicated to food production.

Corn ethanol is the best known and most controversial biofuel. Rising corn prices have a major impact on food prices. Corn is important to the production of a wide range of foods. For example, cattle feed mainly on corn. When corn prices rise, ranchers have to pay more to feed their cattle. Beef prices rise accordingly. The same holds true for chickens and other livestock. The people who suffer most are the consumers, who find their grocery bills skyrocketing.

"[Corn selling at] four dollars a bushel causes a lot of pain," said Richard Lobb, a spokesman for the National Chicken Council. "It ripples right across the economy."

As corn prices rise, more farmers grow more corn. As a result, production of other food crops, such as soybeans, declines. As supplies of these food crops dwindle, their prices rise too.

Much of the world relies on U.S. grain for food. As prices climb, poor people struggle to avoid starving. By 2008 about one-third of all U.S. corn went to ethanol production. Opponents of ethanol argue that using a food crop to make fuel is morally indefensible in a world where millions go hungry.

The criticisms of large-scale biofuel don't end there. Even its status as a green energy technology is in question. To grow corn and other fuel crops, farmers use fertilizers and pesticides that harm water supplies. Ethanol factories use massive amounts of water. Some factories have nearly dried up the local groundwater. In addition, the energy going into crop production—such as tractor fuel—far outstrips any carbon savings.

Opponents argue that the ethanol industry stays afloat strictly through government subsidies (government money invested in the industry to keep ethanol prices down). In 2009 the U.S. government subsidized ethanol at a rate of $.45 per gallon ($.12 per liter). Critics say that while a select few—mainly farmers, manufacturers, and investors—profit from these subsidies, U.S. taxpayers foot the bill.

> "Ethanol production in the state of Iowa has really helped out our corn prices. It's taken a lot of the excess corn that we did have in the state and we've moved it into the biofuel area. Ethanol production has created a lot of jobs."
>
> —IOWA FARMER DENNIS BOGAARDS, 2009

> " **I think [ethanol production] was started with the best of intentions, but the problem with corn ethanol is that it turns out it takes a lot of energy just to grow corn, which we hadn't thought about. The fertilizer, the pesticides, all those things require energy.** "
>
> —**DAVID TILMAN,**
> UNIVERSITY OF MINNESOTA PROFESSOR OF ECOLOGY, 2009

Biomass and biofuel can contribute to U.S. energy independence. But are they really good for the environment? As the United States produces less food, other nations must produce more. In some cases, this means cutting down or burning forests to open up farmland—thus releasing more greenhouse gases into the air than biofuel saves. For these reasons, biomass and biofuel are likely to remain a small part of the U.S. long-term energy strategy.

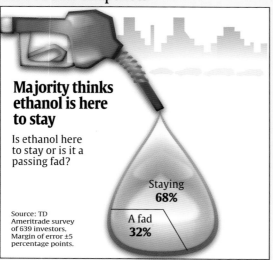

USA TODAY Snapshots®

Majority thinks ethanol is here to stay

Is ethanol here to stay or is it a passing fad?

Source: TD Ameritrade survey of 639 investors. Margin of error ±5 percentage points.

Staying
68%

A fad
32%

By Jae Yang and Julie Snider, USA TODAY, 2006

CHAPTER SEVEN

Water and Earth: Other Alternatives

IN 1992 CHINESE LEADER LI PENG PROPOSED THAT China build the world's largest hydroelectric dam on the Chang Jiang (Yangtze River). The Three Gorges Dam would cost about two hundred billion dollars to build. But when complete, the dam could provide up to 10 percent of China's electricity. In addition, the dam would control flooding downstream.

China's legislature, the National People's Congress, has a history of going along with Chinese leaders' proposals. But this proposal stirred controversy. Many legislators opposed the plan. The dam would create a huge reservoir (artificial lake) upstream, flooding vast tracts of land. The flooding would leave hundreds of thousands of people and countless animals homeless. It would also destroy important archaeological sites.

The proposal ultimately passed—but by the narrowest margin of votes in the Congress's history. According to Li Peng, the building of the dam was

Left: The Three Gorges Dam took more than fifteen years to build. People continue to debate the impact of this dam on the environment and on energy production.

Above: The rising water of the Yangtze River behind the Three Gorges Dam demolished the city of Wushan.

"an event that not only inspires people but demonstrates the greatness of the achievement of China's development."

Construction of the dam started in 1994. Over the next decade, the project forced more than 1.2 million people out of their homes. The reservoir altered the entire regional ecosystem. River flow and flooding patterns changed both upstream and downstream from the dam. Fish populations downstream have plummeted. As a result, the fishing industry has suffered. So have animals that rely on the river's fish for food. Waterborne diseases are on the rise downstream from the dam, because the altered flow of the river has allowed problematic organisms to flourish. Some scientists question whether the reservoir, which sits on several major faults, could trigger earthquakes.

"The function of any river, including the Yangtze, is not only to produce power," said Fan Xiao, a geologist at the Bureau of Geological Exploration and Exploitation of Mineral Resources. "At the very least, [a river] is also important for shipping, alleviating pollution,

The Hoover Dam

The most famous hydroelectric dam in the United States is the Hoover Dam *(below)*. It lies on the Colorado River southeast of Las Vegas, Nevada, on the Arizona border. The dam was the world's largest concrete structure at its completion in 1936. It currently provides much of Las Vegas's power. But the environmental impact of the dam has been severe. Hoover Dam wiped out entire ecosystems upstream and downstream.

sustaining species and ecosystems, and maintaining a natural evolutionary balance. The Yangtze doesn't belong to the Three Gorges Project Development Corporation. It belongs to all of society."

Despite many objections, the dam project continues. It should be operating at full capacity by 2011, producing much-needed electricity for a huge nation. Whether the benefits outweigh the costs remains to be seen.

Water power gets new spark

From the Pages of
USA TODAY

The Holtwood Hydroelectric Dam on the Susquehanna River hasn't changed much since it cranked up in 1910. Workhorses like the 109-megawatt Holtwood, which powers 90,000 homes in the region, have been criticized by environmentalists for the hazard they present to fish. They've been nearly forgotten amid the rush to trendier forms of renewable energy, such as wind and solar. But hydropower—the oldest and by far most widely used alternative energy—is quietly making a comeback spurred by a scramble for clean energy and the high costs of fossil fuels such as coal and natural gas.

Pennsylvania Power and Light is spending $350 million to build a sleek new powerhouse at Holtwood, the first new hydroelectric plant in the East in two decades. It will house just two sets of larger turbines and generators but boast a capacity of 125 megawatts, enough to light 100,000 homes, thanks to new, more efficient technology.

The addition is part of the nation's biggest hydropower expansion since the 1980s. Utilities are proposing more than 70 projects that would boost U.S. hydroelectric capacity by at least 11,000 megawatts, or 11%, over the next decade.

In the early 1900s, hydropower was the dominant source of the country's electricity generation, a status solidified by massive federal projects such as Hoover Dam in the Southwest and Grand Coulee Dam in Washington state. As recently as the 1940s, hydropower accounted for 42% of electricity production. But by the latter part of the century, developers had tapped the most mountainous regions—many in the Northwest—whose steep inclines supply the strongest river flows and permit more cost-efficient projects. Of the 80,000 U.S. dams, only 2,400 have hydro plants. Hydropower today provides 10% of U.S. electricity generation.

But with coal prices doubling since last year, big hydropower additions are now economically viable. Rather than building new dams—which are expensive and time-consuming—developers are adding generators to dams that have none and expanding hydroelectric plants at others.

Another impetus is the growing number of states with renewable energy mandates. Most states recognize new capacity. And since 2005, utilities can get a tax credit for the new power.

"We saw Holtwood as an opportunity to meet (Pennsylvania's) renewable" energy requirement, Holtwood manager Chris Porse says. The Holtwood expansion will also lend a helping hand to migrating fish. Now, shad swimming upstream on the Susquehanna to spawn often can't find the dam's fish lift—a sort of elevator that hoists them above the dam and back into the river—due to strong currents. By siphoning some water to the new turbines and widening the river channel, the project will ease the flow, letting more fish pass, Porse says.

Environmental groups have opposed new dams because they trap sediment and often impede migrating fish such as salmon. But "if you have a dam that's clearly not going away, it makes a lot of sense to look at putting hydropower on" it, says John Seebach, head of American Rivers' Hydropower Reform Campaign.

What other developers are doing:

- **Installing hydropower on existing dams.** Hydro generation is more reliable than wind, which stops when the air is calm. And hydro equipment can generate for 75 years or longer.
- **Replacing existing powerhouses.** Replacing turbines and upgrading generators boost[s] capacity, partly because the angles of the new turbine blades can be adjusted to maximize power.
- **Adding water storage.** Excess grid power at night [can] be used to pump water that's already flowed through the turbines back to the top of the dam for storage. Then, when wind turbines shut off because the air is calm, [a] district can use the stockpiled water to quickly rev up the hydro generators.

Despite the advances, hydropower still can't shake its clouded image. Some states, for instance, allow only small projects to count toward a clean energy mandate to minimize environmental harm.

"It's sort of been relegated to the same position as nuclear," says Douglas Hall, manager of the water energy program for the Idaho National Laboratory. "It's injurious to take that kind of attitude if we're seriously hurting for power."

—Paul Davidson

HYDROELECTRICITY

Hydroelectricity is electricity generated by harnessing moving water. A river flows from high ground to low ground. A hydroelectric plant starts with a dam on a river. The dam creates a reservoir of water upstream. This allows plant operators to control the flow of water. Water pours through openings in the dam. These openings contain turbines. As the water rushes past the turbines, they spin and generate electricity, as wind turbines do.

Hydroelectricity is an attractive energy technology because it is widely available and produces no carbon dioxide or other pollution. It is also extremely efficient and reliable. Hydroelectric plants convert about 90 percent of the kinetic energy they receive into electricity. And their energy production is generally consistent and predictable, unlike some

Above: The inside of the Glen Canyon Dam in Page, Arizona, has eight turbines attached to eight generators.

The Itaipu Dam *(above)* between Brazil and Paraguay was the world's largest hydroelectric dam until the completion of the Three Gorges Dam in China.

other green technologies, such as wind and solar. Supporters say these benefits, combined with the fact that hydroelectric plants are proven and cost effective, make hydroelectricity an important emission-free energy technology.

A hydroelectric plant with a large dam on a large river can produce massive amounts of energy. For example, the Itaipu Dam on the Paraná River between Brazil and Paraguay produces up to 10,000 megawatts of electricity—ten times the amount generated by an average-size coal-fired power plant. The Three Gorges Dam could produce up to 18,000 megawatts.

The biggest drawback of hydroelectricity is its impact on the environment. Damming a river causes flooding that drives both people and domestic animals from their homes. Other plants and animals die. Damming destroys entire ecosystems.

Fish such as salmon pay an especially heavy price for hydroelectricity. Salmon and some other types of ocean fish swim

Above: Salmon swim upstream to lay eggs. Many people worry about the effect of dams on this natural fish population.

up rivers every year to spawn (mate and lay eggs). When a dam blocks a river, the fish cannot reach their spawning grounds and cannot reproduce. This can have disastrous effects on the fish and on ecosystems downstream. Animals that rely on the fish for food go hungry. Commercial fishing also suffers.

Some dams have fish ladders that allow fish to go around a dam. A fish ladder, also called a fishway or fish steps, is a series of low, water-filled steps through which fish can travel to get around a dam. These ladders have been fairly successful, but they don't attract as many breeding fish as free-flowing rivers do.

> " In a world in which the only consideration was the biology of salmon . . . dam breaching [breaking] would probably be the choice most biologists would make. But that's not the world that exists. "
>
> —**BRIAN GORMAN,**
> NATIONAL MARINE FISHERIES SERVICE SPOKESMAN, 1999

Above: A fish ladder runs along the Benneville Dam near Portland, Oregon. Many dams in the northwestern United States have fish ladders for spawning salmon.

OCEAN POWER

Hydroelectric dams are just one way to harness the energy of moving water. Humans have also figured out how to harness the energy from other types of moving water, such as ocean tides and waves. The Electric Power Research Institute estimates that ocean power could provide electricity to up to 10 percent of U.S. homes. That would mean an enormous savings on greenhouse gas emissions.

As the moon circles Earth, its gravity pulls on the water in Earth's oceans. This force creates ocean tides. Sea level rises and falls around the globe, making water rush into and out of coastal areas on a predictable schedule. People can harness tidewaters in much the same way they harness rivers.

Tidal power stations harness the energy of tides using tidal barrages, tidal fences, or tidal turbines. A tidal barrage is a dam across an ocean inlet. Incoming tidewater rushes through a series of sluice gates (openings in the barrage) and spins turbines. The spinning turbines generate electricity. As the tide goes out, the water rushes back through the sluice gates, spinning the turbines again. A tidal fence is an underwater fence with vertical-axis turbines mounted in it. People build tidal fences in areas such as narrow channels between landmasses. Freestanding tidal turbines are usable in areas with strong tidal currents. They work in much the same way as wind turbines.

Tidal energy is clean, carbon-free, reliable, and renewable. Tidal barrages can also protect an area from strong storm surges. A storm surge is a rush of ocean water pushed in by strong winds. Freestanding tidal turbines have little impact on ocean life. And the potential of tidal energy is enormous.

But despite all its promise, tidal power has several

Above: Workers lift a tidal turbine out of the water for testing. This device produces enough electricity for one thousand homes.

❝ The Severn Estuary [mouth of the Severn River] is one of the [United Kingdom's] most important sites for water birds. A barrage would do enormous damage. ❞

—**MARK AVERY,** CONSERVATION DIRECTOR OF THE ROYAL SOCIETY FOR THE PROTECTION OF BIRDS, ON THE PROPOSED CONSTRUCTION OF A TIDAL BARRAGE ON THE SEVERN ESTUARY, 2007

drawbacks. Large-scale tidal power production is available only in a limited number of coastal areas, since technologies such as barrages and tidal fences require narrow channels or inlets. It generates energy only for about eight hours of each day while tides go in and out.

Tidal power technology is also expensive to install and maintain. Ocean turbines must stand up to very harsh conditions, including strong currents and corrosive salt water. A large tidal barrage can drastically change a shoreline, leaving low-lying lands flooded. The structures can also cause a buildup of existing pollutants or salt in the water, endangering local plants and animals. Silt (fine soil) can build up behind a barrage too.

Workers must regularly dredge (pull out) the silt.

Ocean waves, like ocean tides, carry huge amounts of clean, carbon-free, reliable, and renewable energy. People can harness that energy in several different ways: point absorbers, terminator devices, and attenuator systems.

One way to harness wave energy involves a system called a point absorber. With this system, a float is anchored in the ocean. As waves rise and fall, they move the float up and down. That motion turns a small turbine to generate electricity. A single unit (one float-and-turbine pair) is relatively inexpensive to produce. The downside of this method is that each unit produces such a small amount

Above: A boat tows a Pelamis Wave Converter into an estuary in Scotland. The device is a prototype for a large wave farm officials are hoping will supply power to more than twenty thousand homes.

of electricity that it would take thousands of them to produce a significant amount. Therefore, this wave power method might be both too expensive and too labor-intensive to contribute meaningfully to any green energy plan.

A terminator device produces electricity by harnessing wave energy as it hits a shoreline. A tapered channel system (TAPCHAN) is one type of terminator. These systems are built along coastal cliffs. A tapered channel, or funnel, leads into a reservoir. Waves enter the tapered channel. As the channel narrows, the waves get higher and higher. Eventually, they are high enough to wash over the walls of the reservoir. The water collects in the reservoir, and then feeds back into the ocean through a turbine. Gravity pulls the water down through the turbine. The moving water turns the turbine, generating electricity. TAPCHAN systems can produce cheap, reliable energy without any major environmental drawbacks. But the technology works only in very specific locations—those with cliffs—and doesn't lend itself to large-scale energy production.

An attenuator system is yet another method of harnessing wave power. The best-known type of attenuator is the Pelamis Wave Converter. This system is a series of floating cylinders connected by hinges and anchored to the seafloor. As the floating cylinders rise and fall with the waves, they transfer kinetic energy to the hinges. This energy passes to a generator, which turns it into electricity. Such systems are durable and relatively inexpensive to produce. The technology is new, however, and has yet to be used on a large scale.

GEOTHERMAL POWER

Earth holds huge amounts of heat energy from the planet's formation billions of years ago. Earth's interior is so hot that rocks melt into a liquid called magma. Usually, this heat stays buried deep underground. But in places called hot spots, it escapes to the surface. Volcanoes spew magma. Hot springs, such as those at Yellowstone National Park, vent groundwater heated in the depths of Earth.

Below: Iceland is rich in geothermal resources. The Svartsengi Power Plant feeds the country's famous Blue Lagoon. Geothermal energy heats 90 percent of homes and accounts for almost 25 percent of energy usage in Iceland.

Push for geothermal juice picks up steam

From the Pages of
USA TODAY

There's good reason one of the nation's most promising renewable energies is the industry's best-kept secret: It's buried miles under the surface of the Earth. Yet geothermal energy, which taps the Earth's natural heat to generate electricity, is making a big comeback after a decade-long lull. And a recent MIT [Massachusetts Institute of Technology]-led report says geothermal could supply at least 10 percent of U.S. power by 2050, rivaling nuclear and hydropower, if afforded a $1 billion research investment over the next 15 years.

That's because unlike wind and solar energy—both geographically spotty and intermittent sources—geothermal resources theoretically can supply a near-constant underground cauldron of energy almost anywhere. It can even be harnessed in the heart of East Coast cities if developers can find ways to drill deep enough at low cost.

But the industry faces several hurdles, including a Bush administration proposal to ax funding for geothermal research based on a view that the technology is mature. Like oil and natural gas prospectors, geothermal developers use giant rigs to bore deep into the Earth. But instead of mining for fossil fuels, they hunt for hot water to produce steam that turns turbines.

Today, 62 geothermal plants in California, Nevada, Utah, Hawaii and Alaska make up 3 percent of the nation's renewable energy and produce about 0.3 percent of all U.S. power. Seventy-five projects under development in 12 Western states would nearly double current capacity to 5,400 megawatts the next three to five years, enough to light about 4 million homes.

Last week, Calpine announced a $200 million expansion of the Geysers in California, the world's largest geothermal project. Geothermal already supplies 5 percent of California's power.

The 1970s oil crisis sparked a construction flurry, but few projects came online after natural gas prices fell in the early 1990s. The current surge was triggered by high natural gas prices and a scramble for renewable energy to help supply a projected 50 percent increase in U.S. demand for power by 2030. About half the states require utilities to use a percentage of alternative energy for supply. That's likely to increase as Congress looks to limit carbon-dioxide emissions from fossil-fuel plants amid growing concerns about global warming. Geothermal got a further boost in 2005 when Congress gave it the same tax credit wind farms receive.

Geothermal energy harnesses the heat that rises from Earth's white-hot core. In the USA, all projects are in the West, where Earth's shifting plates allow molten rock and water to settle nearest to the surface, letting developers drill no more than a mile or two [1.6 or 3.2 km].

Most geothermal sites are built near obvious signs of resources, such as hot springs or volcanoes. After finding a productive well, developers typically pump roughly 400-degree [F, or 204°C] water into a low-pressure tank, causing it to turn to steam that cranks a turbine.

At the Geysers, water is so hot—up to 600 degrees [F, or 316°C]—that it turns to steam underground, then naturally rises to the surface. Calpine is adding 80 megawatts at the 725-megawatt facility—which powers more than 500,000 homes—partly by drilling and expanding wells.

A relatively new "binary" process can tap 300-degree [F, or 149°C] water that heats another liquid, such as isopentane, that vaporizes at lower temperatures. This lets developers find suitable water in many more places.

But exploration can be arduous. Only one in five wells yields hot water, and each costs a few million dollars. Geothermal energy is also getting tougher to find and extract. Top developer Ormat may partner with oil companies, which often hit hot water accidentally.

The MIT report, funded by the Department of Energy, says future technology could make it cost-effective to drill up to 6 miles [10 km] deep to tap water even in the eastern USA. Other advances include funneling water to sites packed with hot but dry rocks.

DOE has proposed killing geothermal's research funds for fiscal 2008, but spokeswoman Julie Ruggiero says it "would never turn its back on a promising technology." Bills by Senate Energy Committee Chairman Jeff Bingaman, D-N.M., and Rep. Jerry McNerney, D-Calif., would devote up to $500 million to research through 2012.

—Paul Davidson

People can harness geothermal energy in a few different ways. Direct geothermal energy is the simplest. This type of energy is available in areas near hot springs or natural geothermal water reservoirs lying not far underground. Pumps move the hot water directly into homes and businesses for heat. Large geothermal power plants drill into deeper reservoirs, pumping up large amounts of hot water. Steam rising off the hot water turns turbines, which generate electricity. Then pumps return the cooled water back underground, where it reheats and is used again and again.

The geothermal heat pump, by contrast, doesn't rely on geological hot spots. Instead, it takes advantage of the steady temperature of soil and water underground. Just a few feet below Earth's surface, soil and water remain at about 50 to 60°F (10 to 16°C) year-round. A geothermal

Above: Greg Edmundson, principal of a school in Germantown, Maryland, shows off his school's geothermal energy system. The system's pipes descend 500 feet (150 m) and use Earth's natural temperature to heat and cool the school.

heat pump inside a building on the surface circulates fluid from the building to underground and back. During winter the circulated fluid gains heat underground. It carries that heat to the surface and helps warm the building. During summer the fluid carries heat underground and away from the building, helping cool it.

Direct geothermal energy is inexpensive and clean compared to fossil fuel–based energy. However, direct geothermal energy is limited to areas near geological hot spots.

And geothermal drilling is expensive. If the hot water is too far below the surface, the drilling cost can grow too high for energy savings to offset it.

Geothermal heat pumps work almost anywhere. They are efficient and inexpensive and are not limited to geological hot spots. Heat pumps only serve to heat and cool a building, however. They do not provide electricity (and in fact require electricity to operate). That is a minor drawback, however, and the use of geothermal heat pumps is on the rise.

CHAPTER EIGHT

Electric Cars, Hybrids, and Fuel Cells

IN 2003 A SMALL U.S. COMPANY CALLED TESLA MOTORS set out to change the way people think about fuel-efficient cars. Tesla Motors is nothing like the traditional U.S. automaker. The company isn't located in Detroit, Michigan, alongside Ford, General Motors, and the other big automakers. Instead, Tesla is headquartered in California, in the heart of Silicon Valley. This area is known for producing computer equipment and software, not cars.

Tesla Motors' goal was simple: to build an electric car that people actually wanted to drive. Electric cars had been around for years. But most people thought of them as small, bland, low-performance vehicles. Tesla Motors had another idea. Their car would be as stylish as it was efficient. It would perform as well as— or better than—sports cars that run on gasoline. The

Left: Some people think the Tesla Roadster is an exciting leap forward in fuel-efficient driving. Others see only the huge price tag on the all-electric sports car.

company set out to prove that a fully electric car had potential for the future of transportation.

In July 2006, the company was ready. It unveiled the 2007 Tesla Roadster. The Roadster was a slick, stylish machine with great power and handling. Its carbon fiber body was tough but lightweight. Its motor and drivetrain (the parts of a car that transfer power from the engine to the wheels) were completely electric. The car didn't need a drop of gasoline. In fact, it didn't even have a gas tank. Instead, it had about 900 pounds (408 kg) of batteries to store electricity. Owners just had to plug in the Roadster to charge it. A single charge of three and a half hours could carry the car almost 250 miles (402 km).

The Tesla Roadster was a completely new kind of vehicle. It was an electric car that offered people almost everything they wanted—and were used to—in gasoline-powered vehicles.

Above: Martin Eberhard, cofounder of Tesla Motors, displays one of the company's electric motors.

There were a few catches, however. U.S. roads wouldn't quickly fill with shiny new Tesla Roadsters. The company was small, and its production capacity was small too. Waiting lists formed. Most people couldn't even afford to be on the waiting list. The cars used a lot of new, expensive technology. As a result, the Roadster was not affordable to the masses. The

2007 Roadster cost more than one hundred thousand dollars. And on top of that, Tesla said that after about five hundred charges, its batteries would start wearing out and would need replacing.

In other words, the Roadster was indeed a big step forward for electric vehicles. But electric cars still have a long way to go before they can rival gas-powered vehicles.

Above: Heavy traffic in New York City, as in other cities, creates a blanket of smog.

THE PROBLEM

In the United States and other industrialized nations, many people cannot imagine life without their cars. But gas-powered vehicles are thirsty pollution machines. The United States consumes almost 400 million gallons (1.5 billion liters) of gasoline every day—most of it made from imported oil. Automobile exhaust creates blankets of thick smog over many cities. Gas-powered vehicles also contribute a lot of carbon dioxide to the atmosphere. As oil prices rise and pollution mounts, the need for new transportation energy technology becomes more and more pressing.

The United States and other countries have turned to biofuels as a partial solution to the problem. Biofuels such as ethanol work well to power cars and trucks. They burn cleanly and don't introduce new CO_2 into the air. But biofuels have serious drawbacks. Many argue that biofuels are not the solution to our transportation needs. Instead, they should serve as a bridge to new technologies.

A 100 mpg sports car so green it's enviable

From the Pages of USA TODAY

Even as Ferraris, Lamborghinis and Rolls-Royces prowled the avenue, the obscure silver sedan parked at the curb gathered its share of stares and curiosity. The Fisker Karma has looks that rival a Mercedes-Benz roadster. Yet the key to what makes it different is emblazoned on the sides in chrome letters: Plug-in Hybrid. The maker, Fisker Automotive, is trying to carve out a niche in a crowded field of next-generation electric vehicles: a high-performance eco-car loaded with style.

The company has taken more than 1,400 refundable deposits so far for the Karma, which has a starting price of $87,900 and can top $100,000. The car can be driven for 50 miles [80 km] on electric power alone before its auxiliary gasoline engine fires up to generate more juice and extend the range to up to 300 miles [483 km]. The engine never directly drives the wheels.

Depending on the individual owner's daily driving mix, the company boasts, Karma could easily top 100 miles per gallon [42 km per liter]. But the journey from concept to commercial production is not proving any easier for the Fisker than it is for others attempting plug-ins:

- Delays. The Karma's schedule has already been pushed back six months, with deliveries expected to start in June.
- Integration. The company views its area of expertise as design; many of the high-tech components are being outsourced. The approach could complicate integrating pieces from various sources to make sure the whole thing works.
- Affordability. Henrik Fisker, the luxury-car designer who founded the company, says production of a lower-priced, mass-market Karma sibling could be pushed back three years if the company's application for Energy Department loans fails.

Fisker has kept his company largely out of the limelight. Much of the attention involving plug-in electric cars has gone to Tesla and to General Motors, which plans to sell the Chevrolet Volt next year.

The Fisker Karma prototype made its driving debut earlier this month before auto fans gathered for the Rolex Monterey Historic Automobile Races. The lap around the track and the crowd response went so well that executives decided to drive the prototype around and park it on the street to attract attention.

But with its high price, the Karma is aimed at a pretty exclusive club of motorists. And the company has been so low-key that even electric-car advocates aren't sure what to make of the Karma.

Some electric-car experts aren't bothered by Fisker's low-key approach. Having shown the Karma at the big Detroit auto show in January and now having shown that it can tool around a racetrack, Fisker is sticking to the playbook of most automakers.

Fisker Automotive was founded a couple of years ago with seed money from two Silicon Valley venture-capital firms. It since has gone through three rounds to raise more, with total capital of about $100 million as of about six months ago.

Still, that's not going to be enough to retool an auto plant in the U.S. to expand the line with its plug-in mass-market sedan, Fisker says. That's why the company seeks a loan from the government's Advanced Technology Vehicles Manufacturing program. Fisker wouldn't disclose the amount his company is seeking, and the Energy Department says the applications are confidential.

Fisker, he says, will survive without it, but "if we don't get it, we have to wait three years" before the company expects it can raise the money to build the plant for the lower-priced car.

In the meantime, Fisker has plans for two other products that would be built off the upscale Karma's chassis. One is a two-door convertible called the Sunset.

The other isn't being disclosed.

After all, it is a low-key company.

—Chris Woodyard

ELECTRIC CARS

The idea of running a car on electricity rather than gasoline is nothing new. Many early automobiles—before the invention of the internal combustion engine—ran on electricity. Gasoline-powered engines proved more reliable, powerful, and inexpensive to maintain. As a result, the electric car was all but forgotten for most of the 1900s.

Toward the end of the century, people began thinking about electric cars again. In 1990 General Motors unveiled an electric concept car (a car built not for sale but to highlight a new feature or technology) called the Impact. The Impact evolved into the EV1.

But the EV1 and similar cars were not popular, and automakers did little to promote them.

The EVI (*above*), running on battery power, didn't provide enough power to rival gasoline engines.

The cars' biggest problem was energy storage. Their batteries simply were not big enough or powerful enough to provide the energy needed for a driving experience equal to that of gas-powered vehicles. Electric vehicles were slow. They couldn't accelerate quickly. They were fine for short commutes at low speeds, but cross-country trips were prohibitively difficult.

The Tesla Roadster changed the game for electric vehicles. The Roadster performed like a gasoline-powered car, using power stored in its large array of batteries. Despite its high cost, the Roadster helped prove the viability of electric vehicle technology. The Roadster inspired a new wave of research into the electric vehicle. More and more engineers and entrepreneurs are trying to make electric cars both desirable and affordable to the masses.

> **It will take several decades until the market is dominated by electric vehicles. If people are thinking it's going to be like mobile phones, where they went from incredibly expensive status symbols to relatively affordable, commonplace items in a very short time period, then they're wrong.**
>
> **—RICHARD MARSHALL,** ENERGY AND ENVIRONMENT DIRECTOR OF AUSTRALIAN AUTOMAKER HOLDEN, 2009

Electric cars present a unique energy challenge. Most U.S. electricity comes from coal. So electric vehicles are truly green only when their electricity comes from clean, renewable sources, such as solar, wind, or hydropower. But even when electric vehicles get

> " **Even using the worst assumptions for electricity generation, an EV [electric vehicle] is more efficient and less polluting than the gasoline equivalent. If you use best-in-class electricity production . . . , the difference is enormous.** "
>
> **—DARRYL SIRY,** VICE PRESIDENT OF MARKETING, TESLA MOTORS, 2007

their electricity from fossil fuels, they're still greener than gas-powered cars because they use energy much more efficiently.

ENTER THE HYBRID

While some automakers focus on making better, cheaper electric cars, others are working on another solution—the hybrid. A hybrid vehicle uses both electricity and an internal combustion engine.

Here's how a hybrid vehicle works: At low speeds, its gas-burning engine generates electricity. A battery stores this electricity. When the battery has charged up enough, the vehicle stops burning gas and runs on electricity. When battery power dips, or at high speeds requiring lots of energy, the internal combustion engine kicks back in. The result is a vehicle that gets much better fuel mileage than a conventional gas-powered vehicle. Hybrids commonly get more than 40 miles per gallon (17 km per liter) of gas—easily 25 percent better than traditional cars.

The first mass-produced hybrid vehicle was the Toyota Prius. It debuted in 1997 and spawned a wide range of similar vehicles. Even some gas-guzzling sport utility vehicles (SUVs) now have hybrid models.

The Toyota Prius

When people think of hybrid vehicles, the Toyota Prius is usually the first car that comes to mind. Toyota introduced the Prius in Japan in 1997, but it wasn't available internationally until 2001. The Prius set a new standard in fuel efficiency, getting more than 40 miles per gallon (17 km per liter) of gas. When oil and gas prices soared in 2008, U.S. demand for the Prius soared too. Many dealers had waiting lists of several months for the cars.

Above: The release of the Toyota Prius in Japan in 1997 drew the attention of journalists, activists, and car companies around the world.

Critics of hybrids point out that they're not a long-term solution, since they still rely on gasoline. But the vehicles' better fuel mileage lowers pollution and demand for gasoline. For this reason, supporters say, hybrids serve as a good bridge to greener transportation technology.

Sports
SECTION C

April 22, 2009

Toyota hopes history-making pace car can accelerate hybrid sales

From the Pages of USA TODAY

Denny Hamlin didn't break 110 mph [177 km per hour] Tuesday at Lowe's Motor Speedway, but he still was impressed with a car whose speed pales in comparison to that of his Sprint Cup ride [race car]. "I thought it wouldn't take off as well as a combustion engine," Hamlin said after about an hour making laps in a 2009 Toyota Camry Hybrid.... "The pickup was surprising; I'm amazed it takes off as good as anything."

Acceleration was an important feature in winning approval for the vehicle, which will become the first hybrid used as a pace car [the car that the race cars follow on laps before the start of the race] for the duration of a Cup event.

Above: The first official hybrid pace car, the 2009 Toyota Camry, speeds around Lowe's Motor Speedway in Concord, North Carolina, in 2009.

From a standing start at the pit exit in Turn 1, the 187-horsepower, four-cylinder Camry had to reach 100 mph [161 km per hour] by the exit of Turn 2 to satisfy NASCAR's standards for pacing the 600-mile [966 km] event. Ed Laukes, manager for motor sports marketing at Toyota Motor Sales USA, said the approval process took about a year and included an on-track test Toyota passed with flying colors.

Hybrids have competed in the American Le Mans Series. Laukes said Toyota has interest in eventually racing them in NASCAR. "I know it's a ways away, but I wouldn't be surprised down the road sometime if there's hybrid technology in a race," he said.

Hamlin, whose Lowe's appearance was timed to coincide with today's celebration of Earth Day, plans on his next personal car being a Lexus hybrid ("it's smooth and quiet and everything I look for in a daily driver") but would prefer to remain behind the wheel of an internal-combustion-powered car when driving for Joe Gibbs Racing.

"For an everyday street car, it's not as important, but race fans still love the sounds and noise of a combustion engine," Hamlin said. "I'd prefer a stock car [the type of car raced in NASCAR] in knowing how exciting it is to hear the engine roar, but I think NASCAR drivers are embracing the green outlook of hybrids."

Toyota, which has sold more than 1 million hybrids in the USA, is hoping NASCAR fans will embrace hybrids through its marketing of the pace car, which also will appear at Infineon Raceway, Chicagoland Speedway, Watkins Glen International and Martinsville Speedway and in the Oct. 17 race at Lowe's. The car used in the 600 will be given to a fan who finds a "golden can" of Coca-Cola Classic.

"There's stodginess about hybrid technology among the public that we're trying to erase," Laukes said. "This is a way for us to demonstrate the hybrid used on the track is the exact same car you can buy at a showroom."

—Nate Ryan

HYDROGEN FUEL CELLS

Imagine a car that burns a clean, cheap, abundant fuel. The car emits no CO_2. Instead of dangerous pollutants, it releases water as a by-product. This vehicle is not science fiction. It's a hydrogen-powered car.

A hydrogen fuel cell is like a battery that receives a constant feed of fuel. The fuel, hydrogen, is one of the most common elements in the universe. Manufacturers can make hydrogen fuel from water. A process called electrolysis splits water molecules, leaving hydrogen and oxygen molecules. People collect the hydrogen and pump it into a fuel cell. When hydrogen and oxygen combine inside a fuel cell, the chemical reaction releases energy in the form of an electric current.

The hydrogen fuel cell is an appealing transportation technology for several reasons. Hydrogen vehicles could fill up at hydrogen fuel stations just as gas-powered vehicles fill up at gas stations. Burning hydrogen fuel is clean and efficient. It produces no pollutants. And fuel cells are more than 60 percent efficient—far better than gasoline-powered engines.

Hydrogen fuel cells do have their drawbacks, however. It takes energy for hydrogen fuel manufacturers to separate the hydrogen and oxygen in water. That energy has to come from somewhere. It usually comes from burning natural gas. Opponents of hydrogen fuel point out that burning a fossil fuel to create a "clean" energy source isn't solving anything. It's just

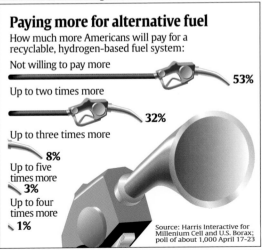

USA TODAY Snapshots®

Paying more for alternative fuel

How much more Americans will pay for a recyclable, hydrogen-based fuel system:

Not willing to pay more — **53%**

Up to two times more — **32%**

Up to three times more — **8%**

Up to five times more — **3%**

Up to four times more — **1%**

Source: Harris Interactive for Millenium Cell and U.S. Borax; poll of about 1,000 April 17–23

By Lori Joseph and Adrienne Lewis, USA TODAY, 2003

Above: This Hyundai Tucson FCEV (fuel cell electric vehicle) contains a hydrogen fuel cell and a backup hybrid battery. It is a test vehicle used to promote hydrogen fuel cell technology and look at its capabilities.

moving the problem around. Fuel cell vehicles are truly green only if they use hydrogen fuel produced by renewable sources of energy.

Another issue that may impact the development of fuel cell vehicles is the availability of hydrogen fuel. Fuel cell vehicles are useful only if filling stations sell hydrogen fuel. It may take a long time before the fuel becomes accessible enough to make fuel cell vehicles practical.

EPILOGUE

Going Green

SCIENTISTS AND SOCIETY GENERALLY AGREE ABOUT the harmful global effects of burning fossil fuels. In addition to those effects, coal, oil, and natural gas are all finite resources. They will run out if people keep burning them for power.

According to most sources, fossil fuels will run out within this century. U.S. oil production volume peaked in 1997, and world production is expected to peak in the 2010s. Even if the world's known oil reserves double through new discoveries, the current usage rate will burn it all up by 2082. The stories are similar for coal and natural gas.

The news is even worse if usage increases. China and India are industrializing. As these huge nations continue to rapidly build industries, their demand for fossil fuels grows. And as they use more and more fossil fuels, the end of the age of fossil fuels draws nearer.

Common sense dictates that people must move toward clean, renewable energy. Will solar, wind, nuclear, and other alternative technologies be ready to

Shown here from space, North America *(left)* isn't the only place that global climate change will affect. It will affect the whole world. But what will going green look like? And when can we afford to go green?

fill the void when fossil fuels run out? They could be, if the world makes a swift and decisive effort to develop green energy.

The transition to a green energy economy will not be easy. In fact, many opponents say that it will be too difficult and too expensive and it will ruin a U.S. economy that's already in tough shape. Fossil fuels are still cheap, and the infrastructure for extracting, transporting, and burning them is already in place. Critics of green energy say we should stick with what's working for now.

Supporters of green energy disagree. They say that the transition is inevitable. The sooner people adopt green technologies, the less painful the transition will be. Supporters point out that green technology development need not strain the economy. In fact, they insist that the transition will help the economy. Green energy

Below: Southern California Edison's Electric Vehicle Technical Center in Pomona, California, displays a Garage of the Future. It has an electric vehicle with charging station and a photovoltaic generator.

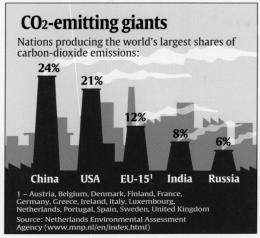

USA TODAY Snapshots®

CO₂-emitting giants

Nations producing the world's largest shares of carbon-dioxide emissions:

24% China
21% USA
12% EU-15[1]
8% India
6% Russia

1 – Austria, Belgium, Denmark, Finland, France, Germany, Greece, Ireland, Italy, Luxembourg, Netherlands, Portugal, Spain, Sweden, United Kingdom

Source: Netherlands Environmental Assessment Agency (www.mnp.nl/en/index.html)

By Anne R. Carey and Veronica Salazar, USA TODAY, 2008

technology will produce booming new industries and many new, well-paying jobs. It will spur the economy much as personal computers and the Internet did in the 1990s.

Nobody knows exactly what shape the United States' energy future will take. Will nuclear fusion become a viable energy source? If so, it may solve all the world's energy problems. Or will cleaner, safer nuclear fission be the answer? Will humans build massive solar arrays in space? Or will we meet our energy needs with a mix of solar, wind, water, nuclear, geothermal, and other green technologies? Only time will tell.

TIMELINE

ca. 800,000 B.C.	Humans discover how to control and use fire.
ca. 3,000 B.C.	The ancient Mesopotamians are using crude oil as a source of light and heat.
600s B.C.	The ancient Greeks discover static electricity by rubbing a silk cloth over an amber rod.
A.D. 1600	William Gibson uses the term *electricus* to compare the attractive powers of magnets and amber.
1646	English physician Thomas Browne coins the term *electricity*.
1752	Benjamin Franklin conducts his famous experiment, proving that electricity is the force that drives lightning.
1769	James Watt builds and patents his famous steam engine.
1870	John D. Rockefeller cofounds the Standard Oil Company.
ca. 1900	Demand for oil rises as gas-burning automobiles become popular.
1920s–1950s	U.S. oil imports triple from 60 million barrels to 180 million barrels.
1934	Enrico Fermi conducts the first nuclear fission experiment.
1936	Construction of the Hoover Dam is completed. The dam becomes the world's largest concrete structure and the world's largest electricity-generating station.
1939–1945	The Manhattan Project develops uranium enrichment facilities, nuclear reactors, and nuclear weapons in the United States.
1945	The United States drops two nuclear bombs on Japan, ending World War II.
1951	An experimental reactor in Idaho produces the world's first nuclear-generated electricity.

1954	The Soviet Union opens a fully functioning nuclear power plant.
1973	OAPEC announces an oil embargo against the United States in response to U.S. military support of Israel. The price of gasoline surges, and shortages follow.
1974	The oil embargo ends.
1979	A short energy crisis results from political instability in Iran. The Three Mile Island nuclear power plant suffers a partial meltdown, causing many to question the safety of nuclear power.
LATE **1970s–** EARLY **1980s**	U.S. solar and wind power enjoy a brief surge in development and popularity.
1986	The world's worst nuclear accident takes place at Chernobyl in the Soviet Union. Fifty-seven people die instantly, and countless more are exposed to radioactive waste.
1990s	Scientific study and public awareness of global climate change intensifies.
1994	China begins construction on the controversial Three Gorges Dam.
1997	U.S. oil production peaks. Eighty-four nations sign the Kyoto Protocol. The United States declines to sign the agreement. Toyota introduces the Prius, the world's first mass-produced hybrid vehicle.
2001	The Toyota Prius becomes available internationally.
2003	Tesla Motors sets out to build a high-performance electric car.
2005	President George W. Bush signs the Energy Policy Act of 2005. Maine officials propose building the controversial Redington Wind Farm.

2006 California lawmakers pass the Million Solar Roofs legislation.

2007 The solar array at Nellis Air Force Base in Nevada begins operation. President Bush signs the Energy Independence and Security Act of 2007.

2008 The price of oil surges to more than $140 per barrel, raising gasoline prices over $4 per gallon ($1.05 per liter). The Wilkins Ice Shelf in Antarctica begins to collapse. About one-third of the U.S. corn harvest goes toward ethanol production.

2009 The administration of President Barack Obama reverses plans to store all U.S. nuclear waste at a site under Nevada's Yucca Mountain, citing geological instability in the region.

GLOSSARY

atmosphere: the blanket of gases that envelops Earth

biofuel: processed biomass

biomass: any living or recently living organic matter that can be burned or otherwise used to generate electricity or heat

carbon dioxide (CO_2): a colorless, odorless gas made of carbon and oxygen; the greenhouse gas that contributes most to Earth's current global warming

carbon sequestration: long-term storage of carbon dioxide, such as by planting trees or by capturing the CO_2 released from burning fossil fuels and then pumping and sealing it deep underground

climate change: a long-term change in the normal climate of one or more regions; the result of Earth's current global warming

E85: a fuel containing 85 percent ethanol and 15 percent gasoline

embargo: a reduction or a halt in trade, often enacted for political reasons

ethanol: ethyl alcohol. Ethanol is a biofuel made from the sugar, starch, or cellulose in plants. Ethanol blended with gasoline fuels internal combustion engines.

flex-fuel vehicle: a vehicle that can burn either regular gasoline or E85

fossil fuel: a fuel formed from organisms buried beneath Earth's surface for millions of years. Coal, oil, and natural gas are fossil fuels.

global warming: a rise in Earth's average surface temperature

greenhouse effect: the trapping of heat radiating from Earth's sun-warmed surface by certain atmospheric gases

greenhouse gas: atmospheric gas, such as carbon dioxide, that traps heat radiating from Earth's surface

hybrid vehicle: a vehicle that uses both electricity and an internal combustion engine

industrialized nation: a nation that uses many energy-driven machines to produce and manufacture goods

internal combustion engine: an engine that burns fuel within itself to produce power

nuclear fission: a reaction in which an atomic nucleus splits, releasing energy in the process. Nuclear power plants and weapons use fission.

nuclear fusion: a reaction in which atomic nuclei combine, releasing energy in the process. Fusion occurs in the core of the sun.

photovoltaic cell: a device that converts solar energy directly into electricity

radioactive: releasing potentially harmful energy during gradual atomic breakdown

renewable: replaceable by nature. Sunlight and wind are renewable resources.

solar thermal system: a device that harnesses the heat of sunlight. A solar thermal system may use the heat to warm water or space, cook food, or generate electricity

subsidies: government funds to help people, institutions, or organizations. A government subsidizes efforts it considers good for the general public.

turbine: an engine in which a rotor spins, turning a shaft, which generates electricity using magnets

uranium: a naturally radioactive metal often used to generate nuclear power

SOURCE NOTES

22   Ronald Bailey, "Energy Independence: The Ever-Receding Mirage,"
     Reason, July 21, 2004, http://www.reason.com/news/show/34845.html
     (August 24, 2009).

26   William H. Kemp, *The Renewable Energy Handbook* (Tamworth, ON:
     Aztext Press, 2005), 4.

31–32   David Rising, "Antarctic Ice Shelf Collapse," *U.S. News and World Report*,
        April 29, 2009, http://www.usnews.com/articles/science/2009/04/29/
        antarctic-ice-shelf-collapse.html (August 24, 2009).

42   Robin Bell, Ken Caldeira, and Stephen Schneider, "The Big Heat," *Discover*,
     June 2009, 38.

43   John Stossel, "The Global Warming Myth?" *ABC News*, April 20, 2007,
     http://abcnews.go.com/2020/Story?id=3061015&page=1 (August 24, 2009).

50   Elizabeth Svoboda, "Back to the Atom," *Discover*, June 2009, 57.

55   Daniel Whitten, "Obama Rejects Nuclear Waste Site after 20-Year Fight,"
     Bloomberg.com, February 26, 2009, http://www.bloomberg.com/apps/
     news?pid=20601130&sid=aoumcQ0grg0M (August 24, 2009).

58   Thor Valdmanis, "Nuclear Power Slides Back onto the Agenda; Energy
     Costs, Geopolitics Brighten Industry's Future," *USA TODAY*, September 27,
     2004.

59   Svoboda, 57.

61–62   Noah Shachtman, "Obama Shines Light on Air Force's Super Solar Array,"
        Wired, May 27, 2009, http://www.wired.com/dangerroom/2009/05/
        obama-shines-light-on-air-forces-super-solar-array (August 24, 2009).

69   Julie Bick, "Up on the Roof, New Jobs in Solar Power," *New York Times*,
     December 13, 2008, http://www.nytimes.com/2008/12/14/jobs/14starts
     .html (August 24, 2009).

74   Breffni O'Rourke, "EU: Where Sunshine Is Abundant, Solar Power Is Often
     Too Expensive," *Radio Free Europe*, March 10, 2004, http://www.rferl.org/
     content/article/1051838.html (August 24, 2009).

75   Kevin Freking, "Feinstein Seeks Block Solar Power from Desert Land,"
     Washington Times, March 21, 2009, http://www.washingtontimes.com/
     news/2009/mar/21/feinstein-seeks-block-solar-power-from-desert-l-1/
     (August 24, 2009).

75   Ibid.

80   Alan Crowell, "Wind Power Fans Controversy," *RenewableEnergyWorld*
     .com, August 11, 2006, http://www.renewableenergyworld.com/rea/news/
     article/2006/08/wind-power-fans-controversy-45691 (August 24, 2009).

83 Tom Catino, "U.S. Senators Flex Muscles on Wind Power, Radar Issue," *Wind Energy News*, August 2, 2006, http://windenergynews.blogspot.com/2006/08/us-senators-flex-muscles-on-wind-power.html (August 24, 2009).

86 James M. Taylor, "Enviro Group Sues Wind Farm to Stop Bird Deaths," *Heartland Institute*, March 1, 2004, http://www.heartland.org/policybot/results/14562/Enviro_Group_Sues_Wind_Farm_to_Stop_Bird_Deaths.html (August 24, 2009).

87 Ibid.

90 Ibid.

94 Cable News Network, "Riots, Instability Spread As Food Prices Skyrocket," *CNN.com*, April 14, 2008, http://www.cnn.com/2008/WORLD/americas/04/14/world.food.crisis (August 24, 2009).

105 Steve Hargreaves, "Calming Ethanol-Crazed Corn Prices," *CNNMoney.com*, January 30, 2007, http://money.cnn.com/2007/01/30/news/economy/corn_ethanol/index.htm (August 24, 2009).

106 MacNeil/Lehrer Productions, "In Iowa, Questions Arise on Impact of Ethanol Production," *PBS Online*, January 28, 2009, http://www.pbs.org/newshour/bb/environment/jan-june09/mixedyield_01-28.html (August 24, 2009).

107 Ibid.

110 James Cox and Antoaneta Bezlova, "The New 'Pride' of China May Be a Monumental Risk," *USA TODAY*, November 7, 1997.

110–111 Mara Hvistendahl, "China's Three Gorges Dam: An Environmental Catastrophe?" *Scientific American*, March 25, 2008, http://www.scientificamerican.com/article.cfm?id=chinas-three-gorges-dam-disaster (August 24, 2009).

116 Fredreka Schouten, "Dam-Breaking Idea Spawns Fierce Debate about Fish," *USA TODAY*, November 24, 1999.

119 Philippe Naugthon, "Severn Barrage Study Alarms Campaigners," *Times* (London), September 25, 2007, http://www.timesonline.co.uk/tol/news/uk/article2531329.ece (August 24, 2009).

133 Softnews Net, "Electric Cars Too Expensive to Replace Gasoline, Says Holden," *AutoEvolution*, June 9, 2009, http://www.autoevolution.com/news/electric-cars-too-expensive-to-replace-gasoline-says-holden-7515.html (August 24, 2009).

134 David Pogue, "Solving the Car-Propulsion Problem," *New York Times*, April 5, 2007, http://pogue.blogs.nytimes.com/2007/04/05/solving-the-car-propulsion-problem/ (August 24, 2009).

SELECTED BIBLIOGRAPHY

Brune, Michael. *Coming Clean: Breaking America's Addiction to Oil and Coal.* San Francisco: Sierra Club Books, 2008.

Carbon, Max W. *Nuclear Power: Villain or Victim? Our Most Misunderstood Source of Electricity.* Madison, WI: Pebble Beach Publishers, 2006.

Casper, Julie Kerr. *Energy: Powering the Past, Present, and Future.* New York: Chelsea House, 2007.

Egendorf, Laura K., ed. *Energy Alternatives.* Detroit: Greenhaven Press, 2006.

Gibilisco, Stan. *Alternative Energy Demystified: A Self-Teaching Guide.* New York: McGraw-Hill, 2007.

Gore, Albert. *An Inconvenient Truth: The Planetary Emergency of Global Warming and What We Can Do about It.* Emmaus, PA: Rodale Press, 2006.

Hoffmann, Peter. *Tomorrow's Energy: Hydrogen, Fuel Cells, and the Prospects for a Cleaner Planet.* Cambridge, MA: MIT Press, 2002.

Kruger, Paul. *Alternative Energy Resources: The Quest for Sustainable Energy.* Hoboken, NJ: John Wiley and Sons, 2006.

Newton, David E. *Nuclear Power.* New York: Facts on File, 2006.

Shuster, Joseph M. *Beyond Fossil Fools: The Roadmap to Energy Independence by 2040.* Edina, MN: Beaver's Pond Press, 2008.

U.S. Government Accountability Office. *Wind Power: Impacts on Wildlife and Government Responsibilities for Regulating Development and Protecting Wildlife.* Washington, DC: U.S. Government Accountability Office, 2005.

ORGANIZATIONS TO CONTACT

American Wind Energy Association (AWEA)
    1501 M Street NW, Suite 1000
    Washington, DC 20005
    202-383-2500
    http://www.awea.org
    AWEA's mission is to promote wind power as a key player in the U.S.
    economy, environment, and energy independence.

Center for Biological Diversity (CBD)
    P.O. Box 710
    Tucson, AZ 85702-0710
    520-623-5252
    http://www.biologicaldiversity.org
    CBD works through science, law, and creative media to secure a future
    for all species on the brink of extinction. This organization supports the
    development of green energy to avoid destroying pristine landscapes.

Geothermal Resources Council (GRC)
    P.O. Box 1350
    2001 Second Street, Suite 5
    Davis, CA 95617-1350
    530-758-2360
    http://www.geothermal.org
    GRC is a nonprofit educational association that encourages worldwide
    development of geothermal resources, promotes research and
    exploration of geothermal energy, and provides unbiased information
    on the nature of geothermal resources.

International Action on Global Warming (IGLO)
    Association of Science-Technology Centers
    1025 Vermont Avenue NW, Suite 500
    Washington, DC 20005-6310
    202-783-7200
    http://astc.org/iglo
    IGLO is a project of the Association of Science-Technology Centers, an
    international organization of science centers and museums dedicated
    to fostering public understanding of science. IGLO's goal is to raise
    public awareness about the impact of global warming.

Renewable Fuels Association (RFA)

One Massachusetts Avenue NW, Suite 820
Washington, DC 20001
202-289-3835
http://www.ethanolrfa.org
As the national trade association for the U.S. ethanol industry, RFA
promotes policies, regulations, and research and development
initiatives that encourage production and use of fuel ethanol.

Solar Electric Power Association (SEPA)

1220 19th Street NW, Suite 401
Washington, DC 20036
202-857-0898
http://www.solarelectricpower.org
SEPA is composed of more than five hundred solar industry,
government, and research members. Its mission is to promote the use
of solar electric power through education, analysis, and networking.

U.S. Department of Energy (DOE)

1000 Independence Avenue SW
Washington, DC 20585
800-342-5363
http://www.energy.gov
DOE's mission is to advance the national, economic, and energy
security of the United States; to promote scientific and technological
innovation in support of that mission; and to ensure the environmental
cleanup of the national nuclear weapons complex.

World Nuclear Association (WNA)

22a Saint James's Square
London SW1Y 4JH
UK
44-0-20-7451-1520
http://www.world-nuclear.org
WNA is a global private-sector organization that seeks to promote
the peaceful worldwide use of nuclear power as a sustainable energy
resource for the coming centuries. Specifically, WNA is concerned
with nuclear power generation and all aspects of the nuclear fuel
cycle, including mining, conversion, enrichment, fuel fabrication, plant
manufacture, transport, and the safe disposal of spent fuel.

FURTHER INFORMATION

BOOKS

Farrar, Amy. *Global Warming*. Edina, MN: ABDO, 2007.
This book explores the path that has led to global climate change, discusses the potential impacts of rising global temperatures, and suggests ways in which humans may avert a global catastrophe.

Gifford, Clive. *Planet Under Pressure: Energy*. Chicago: Heinemann, 2006.
Through text, charts, graphs, and tables, this title shows the impact of energy consumption on planet Earth. Gifford also discusses energy alternatives and looks ahead toward the future of energy.

Gore, Al. *An Inconvenient Truth: The Crisis of Global Warming*. New York: Viking, 2007.
In this juvenile adaptation of his famous book, former U.S. vice president Al Gore discusses the issues surrounding global warming, why it is happening, and what steps people can take to curb it.

Johnson, Rebecca L. *Investigating Climate Change: Scientists' Search for Answers in a Warming World*. Minneapolis: Twenty-First Century Books, 2009.
Johnson explains the scientific investigation of global climate change, laying out the evidence that it is happening and exploring ways to meet the challenge.

Jovinelly, Joann. *Oil: The Economics of Fuel*. New York: Rosen, 2008.
The author discusses the history of oil and its impact on the modern U.S. economy. She also addresses the environmental concerns associated with oil and other fossil fuels and discusses alternative energy sources.

Morgan, Sally. *Alternative Energy Sources*. Chicago: Heinemann, 2009.
Morgan explains the modern fossil fuel–based energy economy and then discusses a variety of alternative sources, including solar, wind, geothermal, nuclear, and more.

Povey, Karen D. *Energy Alternatives*. Detroit: Lucent, 2007.
This book examines the problems caused by traditional fossil fuels and investigates alternatives such as solar, wind, and nuclear power.

Silverstein, Alvin, Virginia Silverstein, and Laura Silverstein Nunn. *Energy*.
    Minneapolis: Twenty-First Century Books, 2009.
    The authors discuss the sources and uses of different types of energy,
    both natural and artificial, including electrical, magnetic, light, heat,
    sound, and nuclear energy.

Sirvaitis, Karen. *Seven Wonders of Green Building Technology*. Minneapolis:
    Twenty-First Century Books, 2010.
    Read about the science and technology behind seven wonders of
    modern green building. Discover everything from earthships to green
    skyscrapers.

Sobha, Geeta. *Green Technology: Earth-Friendly Innovations*. New York:
    Rosen, 2008.
    The author introduces green technology, focusing on solar, wind, and
    biomass. The book discusses why we need green energy and how we
    might apply such technologies in the future.

FILMS

Gore, Al. *An Inconvenient Truth*. DVD. Hollywood, CA: Paramount, 2006.
    In this Academy Award–winning documentary, former U.S. vice
    president Al Gore lays out the case that global warming is real and is a
    serious threat to life as we know it.

WEBSITES

Alternative Energy News Network
    http://www.alternative-energy-news.info
    This site presents the latest news on the alternative energy front to
    raise awareness of and encourage debate over green energy. The site
    sorts news articles by date and covers every conceivable alternative
    energy source. Easy-to-search archives make it a breeze to study up on
    any aspect of alternative energy.

Climate Skeptic

http://www.climate-skeptic.com

Not everyone is convinced that global warming is real. At the Climate Skeptic blog, visitors can read that side of the story. The site is jam-packed with technical information, charts, graphs, news, and commentary—all posted to argue that global warming is not a real threat but merely hype.

Green Energy News

http://www.green-energy-news.com

Learn about the latest breakthroughs in green technology at the Green Energy News home page. Links take readers to stories about wind, solar power, transportation innovations, and much more.

How Nuclear Power Works

http://www.howstuffworks.com/nuclear-power.htm

This site takes the complex process of nuclear fission and breaks it down with easy-to-read text and diagrams. Learn how people achieve and control nuclear fission and about the dangers that come with nuclear power.

HybridCars

http://www.hybridcars.com

Visit this site to see the latest and greatest innovations in hybrid vehicle technology. With pictures, news stories, and product reviews, this is a great site to learn all there is to know about hybrids.

National Geographic: Global Warming

http://environment.nationalgeographic.com/environment/global-warming

On this website, National Geographic offers extensive information about the environment, global warming, alternative energy sources, and more. Text, photos, and video show how global warming is affecting Earth. The site also provides links to related pages.

INDEX

PHOTO ACKNOWLEDGMENTS

The images in this book are used with the permission of: AP Photo/Paul Sakuma, pp. 4–5, 128; © Marwan Ibrahim/AFP/Getty Images, p. 6; © De Agostini/SuperStock, pp. 8–9; © age fotostock/SuperStock, pp. 10, 30–31, 63, 87, 100, 114; © Image Asset Management Ltd./SuperStock, p. 11; © Science and Society/SuperStock, pp. 12, 13, 17, 39; © Karlene Schwartz, pp. 14 (both), 15, 66, 67, 68; © Hulton Archive/ Getty Images, p. 16; © Los Alamos National Laboratory/Time & Life Pictures/Getty Images, p. 18; Photo courtesy of the U.S. Department of Energy, p. 20; © Jason Laure/ Woodfin Camp/Time & Life Pictures/Getty Images, p. 21; © SuperStock/SuperStock, p. 23; © Toru Yamanaka/AFP/Getty Images, p. 27; © Stephen Jaffe/AFP/Getty Images, p. 29; European Space Agency/Press Association via AP Images, p. 32; © Dieter Spannknebel/Stockbyte/Getty Images, p. 33; © Goh Chai Hin/AFP/Getty Images, p. 37; © Patrick Landmann/Getty Images, pp. 48–49; © AFP/Getty Images, p. 52; AP Photo/Jim Mone, p. 53; © Odd Andersen/AFP/Getty Images, p. 54 (top); © Bob Riha, Jr./USA TODAY, p. 55; © Jim Watson/AFP/Getty Images, pp. 60–61; © Rick M. Scibelli/USA TODAY, p. 71; © Luther Linkhart/SuperStock, p. 75; © Wolfgang Kaehler/Alamy, pp. 78–79; © William Glasheen/USA TODAY, p. 80; © Sean Gallup/ Getty Images, p. 81; © Joe Sohm/Visions of America/Digital Vision/Getty Images, p. 82; © Brendan Hoffman/Getty Images for T. Boone Pickens, p. 84; AP Photo/Eric Risberg, p. 90; AP Photo/Ariana Cubillos, pp. 92–93; © Andy King/USA TODAY, p. 94; © Sarah Leen/National Geographic/Getty Images, p. 95; © Prisma/SuperStock, p. 98; © Kambou Sia/AFP/Getty Images, p. 99; © Mandel Ngan/AFP/Getty Images, p. 104; © Du Huaju/Xinhua Press/CORBIS, pp. 108–109; © Keren Su/China Span/Getty Images, p. 110;© NovaStock/SuperStock, p. 111; © Cassio Vasconcellos/SambaPhoto/ LatinContent/Getty Images, p. 115; © Flirt/SuperStock, p. 116; © Tim Matsui/Getty Images, p. 117; Stephen Wilson/Press Association via AP Images, p. 118; © UPPA/ Photoshot, p. 120; © Laura Bly/USA TODAY, p. 121; © H. Darr Beiser/USA TODAY, p. 124; © Jack Gruber/USA TODAY, p. 126; © Robert Deutsch/USA TODAY, p. 129; AP Photo/Paul Sancya, p. 132; AP Photo/Atsushi Tsukada, p. 135; AP Photo/Bridgette Baker, Lowe's Motor Speedway, p. 136; © GIPhotostock/Photo Researchers, Inc., p. 139; © NASA/NOAA/Science Photo Library/Getty Images, pp. 140–141; © Larry Armstrong/USA TODAY, p. 142.

Front cover: © Felipe Rodriguez Fernandez/Photographer's Choice/Getty Images.

ABOUT THE AUTHOR

Matt Doeden is a freelance author and editor living in Minnesota. He's written and edited hundreds of children's books on topics ranging from genetic engineering to rock climbing to monster trucks.